TRANSFORM YOUR
MANAGEMENT
STYLE!

THE PROFESSIONAL PAPERBACK SERIES

The *Professional Paperback Series*, new from Kogan Page, is a major series of practically focused business books aimed at professionals in the middle to senior management bracket. The series covers a wide range of leading edge business topics, including business strategy, organizational theory and design, leadership, marketing, project management and management style. This invaluable series is a mixture of new titles and new or revised editions of best-selling titles. For both practising managers and students of business, the *Professional Paperback Series* will give a boost to their skills and knowledge.

Titles currently available in the series are:

Commonsense Direct Marketing
Fourth edition
Drayton Bird

Transform Your Management Style!
How to Develop and Motivate Your Staff to Achieve Peak Performance
Hilary Walmsley

Total Leadership
How to Inspire and Motivate Through Effective Leadership
Jim Barrett

Designing Organizations
The Foundation for Excellence
Third edition
Philip Sadler

The Top Consultant
Developing Your Skills for Greater Effectiveness
Third edition
Calvert Markham

The Marketing Plan
A Practitioner's Guide
Second edition
John Westwood

Goal Directed Project Management
Second edition
E S Andersen, K V Grude and T Haug

Creating a World Class Organization
Ten Performance Measures of Business Success
Second edition
Bryan D Prescott

PROFESSIONAL
PAPERBACKS

TRANSFORM YOUR MANAGEMENT STYLE!

How to Develop and Motivate Your Staff to Achieve Peak Performance

Hilary Walmsley

INSTITUTE OF DIRECTORS

**KOGAN
PAGE**

LONDON, UK • NEW HAMPSHIRE, USA • NEW DELHI, INDIA

<u>YOURS TO HAVE AND TO HOLD</u>
BUT NOT TO COPY

First published as part of the Professional Paperbacks series in 1998

Kogan Page Limited	Kogan Page Limited
120 Pentonville Road	163 Central Avenue, Suite 4
London	Dover, NH 03820
N1 9JN	USA

The Institute of Directors accepts no responsibility for the opinions expressed by the author of this publication. Readers should consult their advisors before acting on any of the issues raised.

© Hilary Walmsley 1998

British Library Cataloguing in Publication Data
A CIP record for this book is available from the British Library.
ISBN 0 7494 2581 4

Typeset by Saxon Graphics, Derby
Printed and bound in Great Britain by Biddles Ltd, Guildford and King's Lynn

About the author

Hilary Walmsley BSc, MSc, MBA is a management consultant specializing in organizational/management development, human resources and business psychology. She is based in London.

Contents

About the book

As a manager, what is your style of dealing with your staff? Before reading on, stop and think about what you would actually do in the following situations:

- A designer on your team is losing his creative streak.
- Your most successful salesperson has not applied for an open sales team leader position. You think she would make an excellent team leader.
- A staff member approaches you because he is having difficulty getting along with a colleague on a project team.
- You need to meet with one of your staff who has not followed the correct procedure for organizing his holiday period.

Do you always manage situations and solve problems using the same style? Do you stop and think about the approach you are using, or do you habitually attack most challenges in the same mode? Are you aware of the different styles of management available for you to use – for example, various methods of developing and motivating employees – and ways of problem-solving?

Management development today needs to focus on training managers in the *conscious* use of different styles. That is, managers must learn to stop and think about which style they are going to apply to a given situation, and to be cognizant of *why* they have chosen that style. The approach chosen should correspond to the needs of the situation.

There is an increasing awareness of the importance of giving 'people issues' attention and consideration equal to that traditionally given to financial, logistic, and customer issues. The real methods, or 'how to', of addressing people issues, though, are *not* yet well established. Using facilitative skills (such as coaching and counselling) is the most effective

way to implement the modern participative style of management –
empowering your staff in order to get the best results. This is becoming
increasingly essential for achieving peak performance in today's changing work environment. The techniques needed are basic and simple. The
key is knowing first when it is beneficial to apply these skills and,
second, *how* to apply them.

This book will help you as a manager to develop yourself and increase
your performance management effectiveness by revamping your management style.

Names of individuals and organizations in case examples have been
changed in order to protect privacy.

Foreword

Very few of us seem to have the time to read about, learn and practise the skills that we believe we 'ought' to possess, let alone those which at first glance might appear to be peripheral. Hilary Walmsley, therefore, wisely approaches her subject by making some interesting arguments for learning how to use key skills and techniques for developing others. It is probably fair to say that most of us recognize that it is useful, if not essential, to take the time to build up a 'toolbag' of skills and techniques for dealing with the range of personalities and challenging situations we encounter in every area of life. If you don't have time to read her entire book at the moment, Part I alone is well worth skimming through – but do arm yourself with a pencil and notepad! Using a model and process which is logical and easy to remember, Hilary laces her theory with practical and believable illustrations, many of which are drawn from her considerable experience in consulting and running training courses. If you become sufficiently hooked to want to practise the techniques, she makes provision for you by including a number of suitably practical exercises. I thoroughly appreciate the emphasis placed on the useful spin-off effects of the ability to facilitate individuals' development. These skills not only help to empower colleagues and encourage them to accept more personal responsibility, they also have a number of economic advantages and can serve to enhance the reputation of the manager who uses them. After all, who but the most hard-bitten cynic does not want to be thought of as understanding, fair and wise?!

Unlike some other facilitation, coaching/counselling and interpersonal skills exponents, Hilary sensibly recommends that the aim in using such skills is surely to be able to manage in a rounded, balanced manner. She encourages us to believe that it is possible to find ways in which to develop both productivity and people as fully as possible, rather than concentrating on one at the expense of the other.

Having worked in a variety of management positions during the past 30 years I have participated in, witnessed, and heard accounts of what must amount to tens of thousands of situations in which a more constructive outcome could have been achieved if only those of us who wear the label of 'manager' had employed some of these key people-handling skills. Whatever your position on the management ladder or your level of experience, I think you will find *Transform Your Management Style* a useful and enjoyable read. I warmly recommend it to you.

Dr Clive Morton

PART I

Be a 'Conscious' Manager!

1

Conscious Application of Management Styles

EXERCISE 1   What are you managing?

Pick an average week or month of your work life in the past year. What percentage of your time during that period did you spend on making plans for the future? What percentage of your time did you spend producing (or servicing clients)? What percentage of your time did you spend on paperwork? What percentage of your time did you spend developing your staff?

Future planning   _____ per cent
Producing/servicing clients   _____ per cent
Paperwork   _____ per cent
Developing staff   _____ per cent

Employees, in their day-to-day work, need to recognize opportunities, deal with changes, resolve problems, prioritize, and make decisions. As a manager, your effectiveness depends on their ability to do these things. If they are not doing these things effectively then you need to help them, and it will often be more appropriate and constructive to help them facilitatively than by using a more directive style.

Applying a facilitative style allows you to help others without taking on their situation for them. The situation remains with the owner and, as far as is possible, responsibility for it remains with them. Techniques 'borrowed' from psychologists and counsellors can be applied to bring about accelerated growth and development. An encouraging result of consistently adopting this management style is that you are likely to become highly respected and appreciated by your staff, and word may get around about your style.

MANAGEMENT STYLES

EXERCISE 2   Your present problem-solving style

Step 1. Think back to the last five times that you were asked for help by a member of your staff. Write down a brief identification of the situations in the sections marked A below.

Step 2. Try to recall how you handled each situation. Write down what you did, and how you did it in the sections marked B below.

Situations and Your Behaviours

1A. _____

1B. _____

_____

_____

_____

_____

2A. _____

2B. _____

_____

_____

_____

_____

3A. _____

3B. _____

_____

_____

_____

_____

4A. _____

4B. _____

_____

_____

_____

_____

5A. _____

5B. _____

_____

_____

_____

Facilitative techniques are the 'tools' needed to implement the modern 'participative' 'empowering' theories of management style. The model of management styles below (Figure 1.1) illustrates the continuum of possible management styles from the most directive to the most empowering.

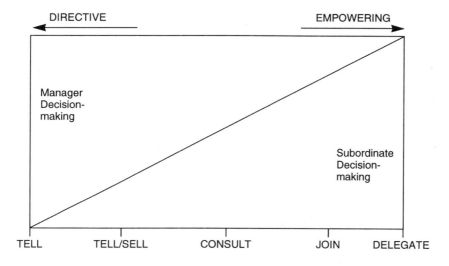

Figure 1.1 Management styles (*Source*: Adapted from Tannenbaum and Schmidt)

'Telling' is being directive about what you want to be done. 'Telling and Selling' is being directive, but taking additional time to sell your decision. 'Consulting' is telling your staff what must be done, but allowing them to help decide how it is done. 'Joining' is deciding together with your staff *what* must be done in order to meet the objective as well as *how* it is to be done. 'Delegating' is letting your staff decide how the objective will be met.

As a manager, you may have very specific ideas about how something ought to be done. The more you let your staff determine how to go about meeting objectives for themselves, the more committed to it they will be. You need to decide on the relative importance of having your own ideas implemented compared with letting them come up with their own, or elect to compromise somewhere in the middle.

The benefits and risks of operating at the opposite ends of the continuum (directive v. empowering) are summarized below.

Advantages of the directive style

- Solutions are the ones that the manager wants.
- If the manager has a sufficient level of expertise, the solutions may be better and more widely accepted.
- Subordinates are clear about manager's expectations.
- Quicker progress and problem resolution (in short term).
- Costs less (in short term).
- Takes less energy (in short term).
- Manager feels in control.

Disadvantages of the directive style

- Encourages subordinate's dependence.
- Brings about compliance, not commitment (subordinates will inevitably be less committed to someone else's ideas and solutions).
- There may be existing unresolved issues.
- Managers will only raise problems to which they have solutions.

Advantages of the empowering style

- Higher level of subordinate commitment to, ownership of, and excitement about decisions or solutions.
- Results in personal growth, development, and independence.
- Subordinate understands solutions.

- In situations where the subordinate has the expertise/knowledge, the solutions will be better.
- Managers may learn from subordinates.
- Builds good working relationship – subordinate feels involved, recognized and respected.
- Can save time, money and effort in the long term.

Disadvantages of the empowering style

- Solutions/ideas may not be as good as those developed by managers.
- Subordinate may not have any ideas.
- Requires initial investment of time, money and energy.
- Subordinate can not view problem in as broad a context as manager.

When you decide to use an empowering style of management, this does not mean you can take a totally hands-off approach, delegating willy-nilly and hoping that all goes well. It is by no means an easy way out. Delegating and operating in a facilitative style means supporting and encouraging employees' growth, which is hard work – but, in the long run, not as hard as having them dependent on you.

Obviously, you cannot do everything in a participative, facilitative, and empowering manner. You must balance the needs of people and the requirements of business, which means developing the ability to shift to different points on the continuum as warranted by the needs of the individual and the situation. Practical considerations and good human relations skills must be integrated.

Blake and Mouton's Leadership Grid is also useful as a framework for analysing your own and others' management styles (see Figure 1.2).

The horizontal dimension of Figure 1.2 measures concern for productivity or for what is necessary for the task to be accomplished – increasing efficiency and output standards. The vertical dimension measures concern for people and relationships, encompassing both physical and psychological well-being. Here we interpret a few of the possible outcomes:

- 9,1 style – Maximum concern for production, minimum concern for people. The manager treats employees like machines, or simply as units in a production process. Scientific or authority/obedience management.
- 1,9 style – Minimum concern for production, maximum concern for people. Focus on human relations and comfort and avoidance of conflict. Manager has happy employees who produce little. Country-club management.

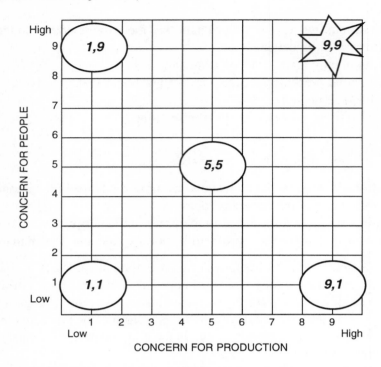

Figure 1.2 The managerial grid (*Source*: The Leadership Grid ® Figure from *Leadership Dilemmas – Group Solutions*, by Robert R. Blake and Anne Adams McCanse (formerly the Managerial Grid Figure by Robert R. Blake and Jane S. Mouton) Houston: Gulf Publishing Company, p. 29. Copyright © 1991, by Scientific Methods Inc. Reproduced by permission of the owners)

- 1,1 style – Minimum concern for production, minimum concern for people. Minimum effort required to get by. Manager plays politics. Apathetic management.
- 5,5 style – Compromise position, balancing people and productivity. Medium concern for both. Manager follows procedures and aims at maximizing production without upsetting people. Not enough emphasis on either people or production to achieve 9,9 position. Mediocre management.
- 9,9 style – The ideal. Achieves highest productivity by gaining utmost commitment. Production through people, making fullest use of all the energy in the system. Team management.

Many managers tend to operate too close to the 9,1 style, unaware of or unwilling to believe that there is a more effective way. Nowadays there are more managers operating in the 5,5 style, where they feel fairly comfortable.

Moving from 5,5 to 9,9 requires an extra-special effort, including the use of facilitative development techniques with individuals and with teams.

ROLE CONFLICT

The previous section intimated possible role conflict. This is the real struggle for managers using facilitative techniques – the conflict with their business task objectives. This task v. people conflict is always there for people in positions of authority and leadership. Good management is knowing when to focus on which. In many cases you will only help to improve work performance by dealing with the people/personal issues. But, where do you draw the line? Different managers will draw the line in different places. A lot of questions are raised over this long-standing debate regarding effective management. It is very important for managers to think through these issues for themselves.

CHOOSING STYLES

How do you decide which management style to apply in a particular situation? Should you use facilitation techniques, should you use your coaching and advising skills, or should you just instruct them what to do? You need to be flexible: move to different points on the grid as different situations require. In many situations a mixture of styles will be necessary and there are, of course, situations where applying a facilitative style would be altogether inappropriate. As a manager, you must always be aware of the different options, make conscious choices between them, and then apply the chosen option with skill and sensitivity.

A facilitative style is often the most difficult for managers to master. The listening and empathy needed for this approach are likely to be difficult to adopt. Managers are used to evaluating and decision-making, and find it easier and quicker to give directive help. They generally feel comfortable (and important) when passing on information, giving advice, or taking over challenges and solving problems on their own.

The best style of helping will depend on four things: the situation, the individual's personality, the manager's personality, and the culture of the company. Below are examples of situations where empowering styles are more likely to be effective and examples of situations where directive styles are more likely to be effective.

Empowering styles are more effective when:

- You are quite sure staff are capable of coming up with workable answers/solutions.
- You don't mind as much about the outcome.
- When a work opportunity/problem is one that could be addressed/resolved in a number of ways, and you do not favour any particular way of resolving it.
- When a decision needs to be made which will have more impact on your staff than on you.
- Your staff have knowledge or expertise which will improve the quality of problem resolution or decision-making.
- It is important that staff have a high level of commitment to the outcome.

Directive (task-oriented) styles are more effective when:

- The member of staff needs your contacts and does not have the power or authority to do something themselves.
- The member of staff does not have the knowledge or capability necessary to solve the problem/spot the opportunity themselves.
- Time/cost limitations prevent you from using a more empowering style.
- The situation is a semi-emergency and fast action is needed.

Even more damaging than being too directive is being manipulative by pretending to be facilitative when you are not. If your employees really understand the concept of facilitation, they will correctly see you as manipulative. If they don't understand facilitation, they may be temporarily fooled, but the long-term result will be at best confusion and at worst suspicion and mistrust. It is better to be honest and open about it when you want to be directive.

EXERCISE 3   Styles of helping

Referring back to some of the examples described on page xi, think about what styles you would apply to the situations outlined.

Of course, your choice of style will depend on the specifics of the situation and the person. Situations such as the three described below will usually call for facilitation because the individual in all these cases knows far more about the situation than you and is likely to be able to come up with some solutions of their own, given a little support.

- A designer on your team is losing his creative streak.
- Your most successful salesperson has not applied for an open sales team leader position. You think she would make an excellent team leader.
- A staff member approaches you because he is having difficulty getting along with a colleague on a project team.

By contrast, the following situation is likely to call for a directive problem-solving method, and instruction giving, because you as manager would probably know more about the procedures than your staff.

- You need to meet with one of your staff who has not followed the correct procedure for organizing his holiday period.

Some situations will call for a mixture of styles to be used. Consider the following case:

- You are receiving complaints from job candidates regarding the interviewing methods of one of your most successful supervisors.

A mixture of facilitative counselling skills with some coaching or training would be appropriate here. This problem needs to be taken care of quickly as it is adversely affecting applicants and therefore also the reputation and image of the company. The supervisor is generally successful so it is possible that all that is needed is training in interviewing skills, but if a facilitative style is used first, you can be more sure of your diagnosis.

Time pressures often push managers into going for quicker solutions (advising or coaching) which may temporarily relieve the situation, but often leave the real issues untouched.

- An insurance broker trainee announces to you that he has missed an exam. Passing the exam is essential if the candidate is to progress and begin dealing with clients.

In the above situation a busy manager might be tempted simply to instruct the trainee on how to register for another test. However, using facilitative questioning and listening skills might reveal further underlying issues which need to be resolved. The trainee might be worried about having chosen the wrong profession, or wondering whether they would be better off in a different division of the company. Overlooking underlying issues can be very costly to yourself and to the company in the long run, so it is often useful to counsel facilitatively before deciding exactly what to do.

In many circumstances, you will need to be directive and firm about an outcome or goal, and only adopt an empowering approach (taking into account staff input and decision-making) regarding *how* that goal is to be brought about. So you may start with certain assumptions and objectives and, working from there, adopt a facilitative style. You need to be clear in your own mind beforehand how much of the decision-making you want to take on yourself and how much you are *really* willing to delegate; and you need to make this very clear to your staff as well.

CASE EXAMPLE 1

Sarah works as a manager for a foreign bank in London. She supervises two sections: office materials/supplies and maintenance. When I met her, Sarah told me that she was sent to see me by her boss, Maria, in order to receive coaching in assertiveness skills. Maria thought that Sarah needed to learn to assert herself more with the three men who worked in maintenance.

As Sarah's description of her struggles with the maintenance department unfolded, it became obvious that she had been under enormous pressures and strain. I used facilitative listening and questioning techniques in order to help her 'tell her story' and help her express emotions of frustration and anger which she had been holding in for a long time.

She was extremely fed up with trying to get cooperation from the maintenance department, who were disgruntled due to their perceived low status within the organization and because they hadn't received a pay rise that year. They tended to take out their frustrations on Sarah by giving her a hard time in subtle – and some not so subtle – ways.

Sarah's style of dealing with them tended to fluctuate between passive (avoidance) and aggressive (loud patronising lectures). However, as we talked I got the impression that she had the capability and know-how to be assertive, but for some reason was not doing so.

Further discussion revealed that although Sarah had responsibility for the productivity of the members of the maintenance department she had no control over their pay, nor their promotions. The authority to give 'rewards' was completely in Maria's hands, although Sarah performed the ongoing and annual appraisals. In such a situation, all the assertiveness in the world would probably not gain cooperation. Sarah needed to recognize the difficulty of her situation, stop blaming herself completely, and be more assertive with her own boss, Maria, regarding management structure and the balance of authority and responsibilities. Fortunately, Sarah recognized this quite quickly and was then able to move on to problem-solving, looking at the options for handling the situation.

We did do some role-plays to help Sarah get back into the habit of being assertive both with her boss, Maria, and with the maintenance men, but this training represented only a small portion of my time spent with her. By counselling her using facilitative listening and questioning skills, I was able to understand the situation fully and to help her begin moving towards resolving it. Had I moved right into teaching Sarah assertiveness techniques, the real crux of the problem may not have come out, and I probably would have been of very little help to her.

EXERCISE 4   Your present problem-solving style

Analyse each situation that you wrote down in Exercise 2. Using the management styles diagrams, try to determine which of the helping styles you adopted in each situation. What were the advantages and disadvantages of using that style? In any of the situations, would a different helping style have been more appropriate? Why? Write down your analyses in the spaces marked C below.

As you think about how you handled the situations, ask yourself the following questions:

- Do I do more listening or talking when staff come to me?
- Do I want to take time out to really listen to people? Or do I try to find a quick fix to get rid of people with problems as quickly as possible?
- Do I always want people to solve their own problems? Do I always want to solve people's problems for them? Or does what I do depend on the situation?
- When I give advice or tell people what to do, is it to save time? To look clever? To look helpful? Do I feel as if I must have an answer to everything?
- Do I feel a need to influence people to my point of view more often than is for the best?
- Do I get to the real issues? Do I get to the bottom of each individual's struggle?

1C. _____

_____

_____

_____

2C. _____
   _____
   _____
   _____

3C. _____
   _____
   _____
   _____

4C. _____
   _____
   _____
   _____

5C. _____
   _____
   _____
   _____

WHEN EMPLOYEES BENEFIT FROM FACILITATIVE INTERVENTION

There are two contexts within which a decision about management style is necessary. One is when someone brings a situation to you. The other is when you have noticed something which may indicate a problem. How do you know when it is appropriate and advantageous to initiate facilitation? Below is a list of such situations (adapted from Reddy, 1987):

- They are not 'mobilising their energies'
  - Not solving problems which they have the resources to solve
  - Not working to a level of which you know they are capable
  - Not making a necessary decision.
- Thinking is clouded.

- Unable to concentrate.
- Not responding to the usual motivators.
- Not taking advantage of an obvious opportunity.
- Engaging in self-defeating behaviour.
- Unusually troubled, tense, or anxious, or irritable.
- Withdrawn from social interaction.
- Poor timekeeping.
- Increased absence.
- Lack of energy and enthusiasm.
- Noticeable unexplained change in behaviour.
- Problematic behavioural patterns
  — Falling asleep in afternoons
  — Drinking excessive alcohol at lunchtime
  — Decrease in performance level.
- Involuntary change occurs
  — New boss
  — Redeployment.
- Behaviour begins to distract others.

CASE EXAMPLE 2

Allan, a manager in charge of a busy sales team, was very worried about a sudden change in one of his salespeople's behaviour. Stephen had always been a keen and energetic member of the team, but recently he had been leaving work early regularly and spending far more time in the private telephone room (a small room with a desk and telephone reserved for employees' personal calls). Stephen was still his cheerful, outgoing self with his clients, but otherwise seemed preoccupied.

Allan decided to approach Stephen to ask whether he could offer any assistance. He suggested they eat lunch together the next day. During lunch, Allan told Stephen that he did not want to pry, but that he had noticed the changes in him and was concerned about whether everything was all right. Stephen paused for a moment and then told Allan that one of his clients had come up with a business idea which he was looking into. He said that he had been keeping quiet about the idea so far as he was unsure as yet of its viability, and of the likelihood of its really coming to fruition. Stephen also commented that he did not know whether the idea would be of sufficient interest to the company, or whether he would need to pursue it on his own.

Allan listened and thanked Stephen for being frank. He agreed with Stephen to meet again the next week to discuss the business idea further. By addressing the situation early on, Allan accomplished several things: making Stephen aware that the changes in his behaviour were noticeable;

giving himself more time to think about whether the company might want to consider being involved in Stephen's idea; giving himself time to consider the possibility of the effects of Stephen's becoming involved in an external business opportunity; giving himself a chance to plan what to do.

2

Managers' Concerns and Apprehensions

OUT OF CONTROL!

Many people fear that they will make things worse by talking about them. In most cases, however, illuminating and discussing problems and opportunities leads to action which makes things better, not worse. You might be concerned that facilitation will open Pandora's box – and that you will then be unable to cope with the consequences. With practice, you will learn to 'contain' the conversation; to set boundaries and limits.

MORE PROBLEMS? NO THANKS!

Operating in an open manner where there is more opportunity for problems to be aired can seem frightening, even stupid, to an already busy manager. However, opportunities ignored and problems withheld will quietly affect productivity and employee effectiveness, and often lead to much bigger problems in the long term. It is wishful thinking to hope that ignoring situations will make them go away – usually, they get worse. But you should be aware that, when you first tackle a problem, things will often get worse *temporarily* before they get better. The initial investment in time that facilitation takes pays off in the long run as staff become more self-reliant and therefore end up demanding less of their manager's time.

JUST LET ME BURY MY HEAD

You may fear that the root of a problem will turn out to be something that you yourself would rather not deal with. The difficulty experienced by an individual employee could indicate a larger organizational issue which you will then feel obliged to address. You may feel uncomfortable at the prospect of having to 'rock the boat' by, for example, having to deal with complaints or allegations against a well-liked senior manager.

GIVE ME AN ANSWER

Another reason managers are reluctant to deal with situations in a facilitative style is because, due to traditional business thinking or conditioning, they think that *they* must find solutions. Managers are often promoted on their ability to solve problems. They are supposed to be innovative in problem-solving. But you do not necessarily need to find a solution or offer advice in order to help someone. You can usually help tremendously simply by being an empathetic listener and questioner. This can often be one of the most difficult lessons for the aspiring facilitator to learn.

WHO, ME?!

You might be afraid that the staff member has a concern about you as a manager. This may be the case. However, it is still better to deal with it than to ignore it. You have the option to either address it yourself with them or to refer them to personnel, whichever seems most appropriate. Although this discussion may be painful in the short term it can, if handled well, avoid larger problems in the long term.

UP, UP, AND AWAY

You might worry that, as a consequence of all this facilitation, the employee will 'self-develop' to the point where they decide to leave the job. However, most of the time having them move on is better than having them stay on either dissatisfied or underperforming. Also, it needs to be mentioned that the nature of your organization itself can deter you from using facilitative techniques to foster employee growth. A quite justifiable fear which prevents managers from developing their employees is that development can lead them out of their own department and onward and upward. There is evidence that, as a result, sometimes managers who are good at developing their staff sometimes hold themselves back. In order to avoid this, organizations need to look at how they appraise the performance of managers and make sure that managers are rewarded, not punished, for developing employees.

To use facilitation skills effectively it is necessary for managers to attain a certain level of maturity and self-awareness, and often cultivate a willingness to change their attitudes, which can be overwhelming or even frightening to some. However, if this fear can be overcome, the potential rewards are great.

PART II

Be a 'Developmental' Manager!

3

Facilitating Others' Development

THE 5-D MODEL FOR COACHING AND COUNSELLING

Many models of the processes for facilitating development have been devised. The 5-D model describes the process in five phases which are easy to remember because they all start with 'D':

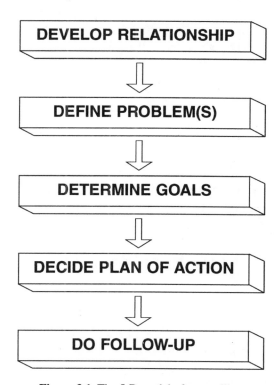

Figure 3.1 The 5-D model of counselling

This process is fluid. Phases do not necessarily follow strictly in this order. You could go back and forth between stages, and you might jump around. In addition, not all the phases are always necessary. You could stop after any phase. Sometimes the initial phases are all that is needed. Having identified the situation and then begun to analyse it, one might be able to make a decision immediately and not need any more assistance.

Facilitation could also start at any point in the process, although earlier phases will either already have been established or will have been quickly reconfirmed. For example, someone might see the situation clearly and know what needs to be done, and yet be unable to act. In this situation you could start at phase 4.

THE PHASES

Developing the relationship

During this initial stage you must create an appropriate atmosphere and establish a special rapport with the individual. Creating a 'safe' environment will encourage them to open up more, to take a closer and more objective look at themselves and, hopefully, to challenge themselves in a way they might not otherwise. The ability to self-criticise is a prerequisite for change and improvement. The conditions which induce people to open up in such a way are referred to by counsellors and coaches as the proper 'attitudes'.

Respect

Respect for your staff is essential if they are to feel confident and gain the strength needed to move forward. Your belief in them is more important than your advice and knowledge in setting up a relationship which will encourage them to change for the better. It is important to make them feel as if they are worth listening to and to treat them as a unique individual, not a case study. This means not jumping to conclusions; rather, try to understand their thinking from *their* point of view.

Genuineness

Genuineness means being real (being yourself) and not putting on a professional facade. It also means being open and showing a real interest in the person. Pretending to be interested doesn't work. Falseness shows through and adversely affects the relationship.

Empathy

Empathy is different from sympathy. It means caring about people and understanding them without necessarily having to take their side, agree with them completely, or become overly involved. Responding to people in an empathetic way will encourage them to progress from talking in a general detached manner to talking in a more personal and direct manner. It can be difficult to retain sufficient distance from a situation if you relate to it personally. Equally, you can be too distant if you can not relate at all. It is important to be aware of both extremes and maintain the right balance between them. Empathizing entails showing that you have (1) heard, (2) understood and (3) accepted (not necessarily agreed with) what they have communicated.

Equality

An equal relationship is necessary for the process to work. It must be a meeting between equal individuals, not a meeting between a manager and a 'subordinate'. This idea of a 'meeting of equals' needs to be established explicitly early on when facilitating, since a manager obviously *does* at other times behave directively.

Listening

It should be established that you are there to listen to *them*. They will be doing most of the talking, especially in the early stages of the process. They will be leading the conversation, not you. This does not mean that you have no input or control whatsoever, nor that you can sit back and take it easy. The kind of listening you will be doing is hard work, as will be explained further in Part III.

You need to avoid changing the topic or taking the conversation in a new direction, except in cases when it is definitely necessary, such as when the employee is waffling, talking in circles, or not talking about what is really significant. In these cases it is best to point out to them what is happening and why you are changing the topic or the direction of the conversation. But generally you need to keep the focus on what is important to them, and let them lead the conversation.

Confidentiality

If confidentiality is an issue, it is very important to set clear boundaries on what will be kept confidential and what will not. Your staff will trust you more if they are clear regarding your confidentiality boundaries. If you ever need to break confidentiality for some reason, this must be explained to them.

The side-effects of working in an environment created by the above attitudes are that the individual gains confidence and independence, enabling them to better approach the situation. Talking about thoughts, feelings and behaviours is a great clarifying process. It sharpens thinking and relieves tension and anxiety. When people think or worry about situations or problems, their thoughts are often vague. Amorphous, partially-formed ideas, fears, hopes, and images float around in their heads, often not in any logical or sensible order. Having to put them into words in a way which will make sense to someone else helps the person to identify and clarify the opportunity/problem and make more sense of the situation.

Defining the situation, problem, or opportunity

During this phase, the situation is defined first by the member of staff from their point of view. The situation will then often need to be redefined more objectively before moving on towards resolution. However, it is important to show that you understand a situation from their point of view *before* challenging them to look at it differently or more objectively.

The point of view

You are seeking to define and understand the situation clearly *from the other person's frame of reference* and also to show acceptance of their view, even if you don't agree with it. Demonstration of understanding is achieved by using a skill called reflecting.

Focusing and prioritizing

You may need to encourage the person to talk about their most significant hopes and concerns, ie the ones having the most significant effect on their work. This may mean helping them to organize the issues. People may throw a lot of confused talk at you, some related to the main issues and some not. In these cases you need to help them to sort out the issues.

A new perspective

People frequently need to gain a more objective view of a situation before they can move on to finding productive ways of managing it. They might initially describe a problem or challenge as being impossible, insoluble, or as being someone else's problem or fault:

> There is nothing I can do about the situation. I am stuck. I have no control over company policy or management decisions so there is nothing I can do to improve the situation.

> She just doesn't like me. She is always trying to make my life difficult. She needs to learn to be more responsible.

Having accepted and understood their original point of view, you can then challenge the employee to look at the situation from different angles or to consider other points of view.

Acceptance

The employee needs to accept that a situation or problem actually exists before they will be motivated to do something about it. There is no point in using facilitation skills with someone to help them to address or achieve something which they do not believe to be an important issue.

Ownership

Having accepted the existence of the situation, the next step is accepting ownership of the problem/challenge. Ownership is a key concept, because it leads to self-responsibility. Ownership means acknowledging that the situation is affecting them, belongs to them, and that they, therefore, need to decide what to do about it.

Self-responsibility

You will need to be vigilant against dependency, especially at first. Your staff are likely to try to get you to give them answers. Get them to help themselves as much as possible. It is a good idea to talk about the dependency/self-responsibility issue openly. Keeping the situation analysis and solution generation in the hands of the owners is the basic concept behind effective facilitation. They need to accept responsibility both for the situation and for doing something about it, which means recognizing that you are not going to take over for them. When facilitating, do not allow yourself to be forced or tempted into producing quick and easy answers.

Consider the difference between the following two interactions:

Interaction 1

Manager:	'Right, that's the situation. What now?'
Subordinate:	'Well, uh, what do you think I should do about it?'
Manager:	'This is what you do. First you..., then you..., and finally you...'
Subordinate:	'All right. Thank you.'

After this interchange, the 'subordinate' might well leave feeling delighted to have an 'answer'. However, there are other possible outcomes. He or she could leave thinking, 'That was a lot of use; I knew all that before I went in' or, 'That might be what s/he wants, but I'm going to do it my way.'

In the second version of the interchange, responsibility for the situation is put back where it belongs, with its owner, so that they themselves work through it to a solution as much as is possible.

Interaction 2

Manager:	'Right, that's the situation. What now?'
Subordinate:	'Well, uh, what do you think I should do?'
Manager:	'You must have given some thought to the possible solutions. Have you any ideas yourself?'
Subordinate:	'I'm not sure, but one thing we might be able to do is ...'
Manager:	'OK, that's one solution. Is that the only one or are there any other possible approaches?'
Subordinate:	'Well, I did think that perhaps ...'
Manager:	'Good. Any others?'
Subordinate:	'No. I can't think of any more.'
Manager:	'We could always have a look at ...' or 'Would it be possible to ...?' or 'Could you consider ...?'

Determining goal(s)

During this phase, the employee will establish goals. They need to decide what they want to achieve or change, and they need to consider what can be improved or 'solved' as opposed to what can only be 'managed' differently.

Choosing and prioritizing goals and objectives

This topic will be discussed in more detail in the section on problem-solving skills. For now, suffice it to say that general goals need to be determined and then broken down into workable objectives. Objectives must be prioritized, and realistic time frames for meeting them considered. Some situations (such as an immediate difficulty with a client) are short term, while others (such as a desired change in career direction) need to be looked at over the longer term.

Commitment

They must be committed to the goal(s). Otherwise, they are unlikely to carry out the plans decided upon. The level of commitment and the need for it may need to be discussed rather than taken for granted.

Deciding the plan of action

For each objective, a specific and workable plan of action needs to be devised. To be workable, the plan must fit in with their life plan, goals, values, and be practicable within the time they have available.

Generating and exploring alternatives

Your staff may need encouragement or even help in exploring the range of options open to them. You might need to remind them to consider that there *are* options, for example:

Manager: 'You have expressed concern about liaising and communicating with the shipping department managers. What do you think can be done about it?'

They may say they want to consider options, but don't know what options are open to them. You need to decide how much of your own assistance is appropriate. You may make suggestions yourself, offer alternative sources of information (literature, another knowledgeable person, etc), or you can continue to probe the person for their own suggestions.

Encourage them to consider *all* the options, even the ones they are tempted to rule out immediately, in order to examine *why* they are being dismissed. The reasons for ignoring or dismissing options can be significant. An alternative which is ruled out initially sometimes turns out to be the one eventually chosen. There is another reason for considering all the actionable options available: it is useful to have fallback plans if the first-choice option does not work out.

Decision-making

Reluctance or difficulty in making a decision can be a barrier to moving forward. Methods for assisting in learning decision-making skills are introduced in Part III.

Specific steps

Once a decision has been made regarding the strategy option, the strategy needs to be broken down into specific steps to be taken. The employee may be tempted to leap into action with only a broad strategy to guide them, but the action is much more likely to be effective if each step is planned and considered carefully beforehand.

Doing the follow-up

The phase of facilitation which is easiest to overlook is making sure that the action plan gets implemented. Members of staff will need to be taught, encouraged and reminded to manage monitoring (looking at indicators of progress), support provision, and incentive provision for themselves. However, you can check with them at regular intervals to 'see how it's going', and make yourself available for back-up support, especially when it comes to helping them to work through any blocks. Depending on how directly related the change is to your own objectives as manager, you may want to arrange regular follow-up meetings anyway.

All talk and no action

Some people may be a bit too comfortable in 'chat' mode, preferring to complain about a situation than actually do anything about it. Throughout the facilitative process, even during the first phase of empathetic listening, the manager must establish the expectation that the meetings are aimed at actually addressing things rather than just talking about them.

Several precautions can be taken in order to facilitate action and avoid 'all talk, no action' syndrome. Opening the meeting with statements which set expectations and time limits will help focus the minds of the participants. While they are determining the steps of their action plans, encourage them to think ahead: What resources will be needed? What might impede the implementation of the action plan? How could these impediments be minimized? Have them plan ahead for the provision of motivating incentives. Another source (or sources) of support may be necessary in cases where change is not going to be an easy process.

The following is a simplified example of how someone might work through the five phases.

Phase 1 – Developing the relationship

- The employee described his colleagues' behaviour (failure to involve him in decision-making process, excluding him from the grapevine).
- Discussed feelings (anger, isolation, resentment).

Phase 2 – Defining the problem

- As he sees it initially, others are excluding him.
- Further discussion reveals that his workstation is physically isolated relative to his colleagues.
- It emerges that he may be contributing to the problem by not listening well and being forgetful.
- Problem redefined as general communication difficulties.

Phase 3 – Determining goals

- Find new ways to receive information which is being disseminated around the office.
- Improve the employee's listening and remembering skills.
- Change workstation.

Phase 4 – Deciding on a plan of action

- Determine the specific steps involved in devising and proposing a new system for the distribution of memos.

- Request a change of workstation next time someone leaves.
- Determine the steps which need to be taken in order to obtain communications skills training.

Phase 5 – Following-up

- Meet with the manager a week later to discuss progress so far.
- Two weeks later, the manager should approach him to see whether his situation has improved.

Part II has looked at the various phases of the process of facilitative helping. You should now have an understanding of how the process works and the appropriate attitudes needed to create an atmosphere conducive to using facilitation skills. It is the *combination* of the attitudes and skills together which make a facilitative style of management work. Attitude alone is not enough; but applying the skills without the right attitudes won't work either. Part III looks at the specific skills you will need to master.

PART III

Be a Manager with 'Positive Impact'

4

Listening Techniques

Listening is the *most* important skill needed in order to facilitate effectively. There are four basic types of things you will need to listen for (Egan, 1990):

1. Experiences: What does the person see as happening to them?
2. Behaviours: What do they do or fail to do?
3. Sentiments: What are their feelings and emotions?
4. Points of view.

Active (as opposed to passive) listening has many positive effects:

- Builds rapport.
- Helps employees to express themselves.
- Encourages employees to feel that you are there for them.
- Makes employees feel heard, understood, and accepted.
- Makes you more influential – listening builds trust. If employees feel heard, they will in turn listen to you.
- Helps employees to address issues for themselves.

Focus on making sure that you have really heard what they have said, even when it is annoying or uncomfortable, and however much you disagree. You must also encourage the discussion of feelings – acknowledge feelings, rather than driving them away. This can be very difficult for managers who are not comfortable discussing feelings, and are not comfortable listening attentively to attitudes and opinions with which they disagree. But unexpressed and unacknowledged feelings can often become a block to moving on.

Most of us are not really very good listeners at all. Despite the fact that as adults we spend the largest percentage of our time listening, as school children we are taught a tremendous amount about reading and writing, a bit about speaking, and very little about listening. Given our lack of train-ing, it is not surprising that our listening skills are not very well developed.

The concept of active rather than passive listening is important because most people consider listening to be a passive receiving activity. Real active listening is hard work and very tiring because it requires an extremely high level of concentration. Unlike reading, where you can go over a passage again and again, when you are listening you have only one chance.

Listening can be broken down into a variety of component skills:

- Reading body language.
- Listening to the *way* things are said (the sound of the voice and the words chosen).
- Being able to see through their conversational style and vocabulary in order to follow the thoughts and emotions that lie behind the words.
- Trying to understand their values and way of thinking.
- Noticing what is *not* being said.
- Listening to the parts and the whole at the same time: learning to high-light the important things in one's own mind as they speak, and to think about how these might relate to one another, and to try to put them together to form a meaningful whole, or concept.
- Becoming familiar with their normal speech pattern so that you can pick up on anomalies which may indicate areas of importance.
- Practising self-discipline in order to eliminate distractions, overcome boredom, and concentrate on what is being said all the way through to the ends of the sentences.
- Demonstrating both verbally and non-verbally that you are listening.

NON-VERBAL LISTENING

According to communications specialists, people communicate far more through posture, gestures and expressions (body language) and with the way the voice sounds than through actual words.

Gestures/expressions	55%
Voice	38%
Words	7%
Total communication	100%

(Figures from study by Albert Mehrabian)

Most people are not aware how much they communicate to others through their body language and tone of voice. Nor are they aware how much they are, often subconsciously, picking up from others' non-verbal communication. For example, if you ask me whether I am excited about my new job and I respond by looking at the ground, shifting my feet, and saying in a dull tone 'Oh yes, I am looking forward to it', which would you believe – my words, or my tone of voice and body language? Most people would interpret my response as meaning I was *not* thrilled about my new job, but reluctant to say so.

In order to best understand people, we need to pay attention to all three components of their communication: body language, words, and tone of voice. Because of its enormous impact, body language is very important. You will be able to communicate much more effectively if you are conscious of your own body language, and you will be able to increase your understanding of others and what they *really* think and feel if you learn to interpret their body language.

It is useful to stop and think about how you would like someone to behave towards you if you approached them for help. How would you like to be treated? Think about what a difference it makes when someone listens really attentively and encourages you compared with someone who seems preoccupied, bored, or in a hurry.

EXERCISE 5   Body language awareness

Think of times when you have felt that someone was listening very attentively to you and really cared about what you had to say. Make a list of the non-verbal behaviours portrayed which led you to believe that they were interested:

_____

_____

_____

_____

_____

_____

_____

continued overleaf

Exercise 5 *continued*

Next, think of times when you have felt that you were not receiving someone's full attention. Make a list of behaviours which betrayed their lack of
interest:

_____

_____

_____

_____

_____

_____

_____

Body language

It is especially important to maintain attentive body language when you are
using facilitative techniques in order to demonstrate attentiveness and communicate a positive and encouraging attitude. Do not underestimate the positive effects of giving someone your complete undivided attention. They will
feel respected and as if they are worth listening to, which will encourage
them to open up and say more. They will also feel free to set the pace of the
conversation and to take their time, helping them to clarify their thinking.

Remember that talking to someone who seems not to be paying you their
full attention has very negative effects. You feel small and unimportant,
which may make you angry and/or upset. Your thinking becomes distracted
and confused. You lose your train of thought and you may want to finish
what you are saying as quickly as possible, even if that means leaving
important things out.

These are the most important non-verbal indicators of attentiveness:

- Eye contact – Plenty of it, but avoid staring. Shows interest, concern.
- Nodding – Acknowledges the speaker's words. Encourages them to
  continue. Nod at the end of the speaker's phrases, not on top of their
  speech.
- Facial expressions – Should be appropriate to what is being said. Shows
  that you are following the thread of the discussion and empathizing.
  Demonstrates interest.

- General manner and bearing – Withdrawn, nervous, aggressive, defensive, passive or not.
- Pulling on the collar, and putting the hand over or near the mouth or nose can be indicative of lying or nervousness.

It is important to look at groups of body language signs together, and not to make assumptions based on one indicator alone. It is easy to lose credibility by rigidly following over-simplistic body language rules. For example, having one's arms and legs tightly crossed does not always indicate defensiveness. It could indicate coldness, or a need to use the toilet. The meaning of body language can also be culture dependent. Below is a useful chart of some non-verbal cues.

Table 4.3 Non-verbal cues

Non-verbal cue	Anger	Happiness	Sadness	Anxiety
Tone of voice	Harsh	Warm Excited	Soft	Timid Hesitant
Voice volume	Loud	Easy to hear Shouting for joy	Quiet	Quiet
Eye contact	Direct	Direct	Averted	Averted Very intermittent
Facial expression	Clenched teeth	Grinning Open	Tearful Mouth turned down	Forced smile
Posture	Rigid	Relaxed	Slouched	Tense
Gestures	Fist clenched Finger pointing	Bouncy movement Jumping for joy	Holds head in arms	Finger tapping

Source: Adapted from Nelson-Jones

Vocal messages

The sound of the voice tells you a lot about the speaker's feelings. Some of the most significant variations in voice include:

- Volume – loud or quiet.
- Pace – slow or fast.

- Clarity – enunciation of words (affected or perfectionist, slurred or mumbled).
- Pitch – high or low, intense or relaxed.

Sometimes people's speech is totally muddled and incomprehensible and therefore difficult to follow, which can, in itself, be useful information.

EXERCISE 8   Listening to non-verbal communication

Make a list of the body language signals and/or vocal messages which can give you additional or different information to what is conveyed by the words themselves. Think of occasions when you have learned more about someone from their body language or the sound of their voice than from what they said, and times when someone's body language/vocal messages indicated to you that what they were saying was not the full truth. What were the specific behaviours which gave them away?

VERBAL LISTENING

By now you should be convinced of the importance of body language. It is also necessary to verbally indicate that you are listening. This section discusses several ways in which this can be done: using encouragers; echoing and key word repetition; reflecting; and summarizing.

Encouragers

The most common way of demonstrating verbally that you are listening is by using 'encouragers': Encouragers are the short phrases and noises we make to tell people that we are listening, that we are interested, and that we want them to continue. Encouragers are minimal responses – enough to show that we are paying attention and not daydreaming, without distracting the speaker.

If encouragers are too infrequent, the speaker will start to question our attention level. While using encouragers frequently is, of course, encouraging, overdoing it can sound artificial and distracting, and actually suggests that you are not listening. It sounds better to the speaker if we vary the encouragers we use, rather than monotonously repeating the same one over and over again. As with nodding (a *non-verbal* encourager), the timing of encouragers makes a difference too. It is best to encourage at the end of a speaker's phrases, in response, rather than speaking over them, which is an interruption.

Following are some of the most commonly used encouragers:

- Umm-hmm...
- Mhmm...
- I see...
- Right...
- That's interesting...
- Yes...

EXERCISE 9   Encouragers

Find a way to monitor your normal listening during a conversation (tape recorder, friendly observer, or self-monitor). Find out which encouragers you use, and how often you use them. Could you sound more attentive by using either more or less encouragers, or a wider variety of encouragers?

Echoing and key word repetition

As well as demonstrating listening, echoing and repeating key words are gentle ways of asking probing questions and directing the conversation. Echoing is simply repeating the last few words spoken, and key word repetition is picking out important words from the speaker's statements and repeating them.

For example, if someone says 'Last year's European conference was not worth the trouble. The hotel was uncomfortable, the conference planners were disorganised, and we sent several salespeople leaving our office short-staffed. However, Roger doesn't agree with me', an example of echoing would be, 'Roger doesn't agree with you?' and an example of key-wording would be, 'The planners were disorganised?'

Both of these examples demonstrate listening: they both encourage the person to continue speaking, yet they both subtly direct the conversation as well and therefore should be used carefully.

Reflecting

As well as encouraging speakers to continue, verbal listening can communicate to them your understanding of what has been said. Reflecting is a way of showing understanding without either agreeing or disagreeing. Part II of this book talked about the importance of attitude. Reflecting is a way of showing non-judgmental understanding and acceptance without becoming over-involved in the situation yourself. Reflecting demonstrates empathy and unconditional positive regard as well as listening.

So what exactly is reflecting? It means playing back to someone in your own words what they have communicated to you. The difference between reflecting and paraphrasing is that reflecting plays back the *total* message communicated to you (reflecting what you have learned from a combination of the verbal content, the sound of their voice, and their body language) whereas paraphrasing plays back just the verbal part of their message. In the example below Manager 1 is playing back the verbal content of what the subordinate has said, while Manager 2 is playing back the total communication.

Subordinate (looking downward):
>'I have been asked to apply for that next grade position which was advertised. It looks interesting (sounding unconvinced). Apparently I have all the qualifications necessary. I ought to apply (annoyed tone of voice).'

Manager 1 (paraphrasing):
>'You think you should apply for a position for which you have been specifically asked to apply due to your qualifications.'

Subordinate (looking downward):
>'I have been asked to apply for that next grade position which was advertised. It looks interesting (sounding unconvinced). Apparently I have all the qualifications necessary. I ought to apply (annoyed tone of voice).'

Manager 2 (reflecting):
>'You sound as if you are somewhat reluctant about applying for this position, but feel you ought to because it was requested.'

Reflecting total communication is often more helpful than reflecting verbal communication only. Manager 1 has understood what the subordinate said, but Manager 2 has given the subordinate some feedback and offered an opportunity to explore the situation more deeply, as well as showing understanding of what was said. The subordinate is more likely to feel better understood by Manager 2.

By choosing carefully which bits of people's speech to reflect, you can direct the conversation. This must be done with care, because facilitated conversations should generally be led by the other person. You can direct the conversation when it will help them to go in a direction which is *important to them*. This is different from taking control of the conversation for your own purposes. Manager 2 in the example above focused on the subordinate's reluctance because the subordinate's total communication indicated that this was an important issue. Manager 2 is not manipulating the conversation. Rather, the subordinate is being encouraged to elaborate on an emotion which is obviously significant to them.

You can reflect emotion, thinking and/or behaviour. It is best to try to reflect as many of these as possible in a reflective statement in order to communicate full understanding.

Supervisor: 'My head technician, James, has been doing steadily excellent work for some time now. He also trains the newer staff in a very positive manner, which boosts their morale at a critical time. In order to keep him motivated, I need to do something more than just giving him praise, yet there is not another position between his and mine for him to aspire to.'

Manager: 'You have been rewarding James with good reviews, but you are concerned because you think something more may be needed to keep him motivated over time.'

The manager reflected the feeling (concern), the thinking (needing more motivation) and the behaviour (praise).

Sometimes it is useful to reflect back on the emotions which are *not* being communicated verbally, especially when the person speaking is obviously avoiding discussing feelings. Thinking and behaviours are more often readily communicated verbally, whereas emotions are more often implied, or communicated non-verbally. For example, the statement, 'I think I am being taken advantage of', implies anger and an accompanying angry tone of voice or thumping the table to communicate anger. Reflecting feelings and emotions is a very important facilitation skill because emotions are often a block to progress. Reflecting is a way of bringing them out into the open and discussing them, so that progress can be made. Simple statements such as, 'You seem upset by this', 'You don't look so happy', or 'You seem quite worried' can help to get people talking about their emotions.

Managers are often sceptical about reflecting when it is explained to them, and express doubts about its usefulness – until they either try it out themselves, or watch someone else doing it well. Then they begin to appreciate its multiple benefits. Reflecting is an extremely useful skill which can have many benefits for both the listener (reflector) and the speaker.

Benefits to reflector (manager/listener)

- Demonstrates listening.
- Checks for understanding and builds a clearer mental picture.
- Builds rapport.
- Paces the conversation – gives you and the speaker time to think about where to go next.
- You can contribute to the conversation without leading it.
- Sharing responsibility – very useful for putting the situation back in their hands (avoiding taking it on for them).
- Forces concentrated listening.
- Encourages opening up, looking deeper into things.

Benefits to speaker

- Helps speaker to 'hear themselves' and therefore keep on track.
- Gain feedback about themselves, leading to greater self-understanding.
- Feel listened to, validated, reassured and accepted.
- Feel understood and/or have the opportunity to correct listener if mis-understanding arises.
- Hearing themselves more objectively through someone else helps to put thinking in perspective.
- Clears and focuses thinking.
- Helps them to tell their story.
- Allows them to set the pace.
- Allows them to come up with their own realizations/solutions.

People have very different conversational styles. Some of us reflect naturally in ordinary conversation. Others never reflect, tending instead to give other types of responses. Exercise 10 is a questionnaire devised to help you to recognise your natural style.

Fill out the questionnaire, choosing the responses to the statements that are closest to those you would give in ordinary conversation (forget about the facilitating situation temporarily while filling out this particular questionnaire).

EXERCISE 10 Typical response inventory

Based on the work of Carl Rogers, this inventory exercise is designed to find out what sort of responses you tend to give naturally in normal conversation. Read each statement and choose the *one* of the five responses given which is *most* similar to the response you would be likely to give in everyday conversation.

Statement 1 (from man, aged 35): 'I have a lot of ambition. Every job I've had I've been successful at, and I intend to be successful here even if it means walking over a few people to do so. I'm going to prove myself and really go places.'

Choose one of the following responses:
A. 'You feel you are a very ambitious man, is that right?'
B. 'Why do you think you have such strong needs for success?'
C. 'That's good. You should soon get to the top with that attitude. Let me know if I can help you in any way.'
D. 'It seems to me that your need for success is so strong that you don't care about being liked by people.'
E. 'It will make you very unpopular here if you maintain that attitude. That's not how we do things here at all.'

Statement 2 (from woman, aged 26): 'Two years at business school have really equipped me to be a professional manager. Competing with men there has convinced me that women who get as far as I have are more than a match for most men. If this organization wants to keep me they'll have to fit in with my own career progression.'

Choose one of the following responses:
A. 'A business school education is a great asset, but if you ask me it doesn't make you a good manager. You have to learn the hard way.'
B. 'What difficulties do you foresee in being female in this organization?'
C. 'I'm sure you're right. We are really in need of people with your skills and drive. Let's get together next week and I'll help you plan out how you can get the experience you want in this department in the shortest possible time.'
D. 'If I'm hearing you correctly, you feel that you are well equipped as a professional manager and you expect the organization to respect this.'
E. 'It appears to me that you have some worries about being accorded the status you think you deserve.'

Statement 3 (from man, aged 44): 'I used to be very ambitious but, as I've got older, success is not so important to me. I may not have been a success with the company, but I've put all my real effort into my family. I'm a very happy family man.'

Choose one of the following responses:
A. 'That sounds like a very sensible attitude. After all, very few people get to the top. Is there any help I can give you?'
B. 'Yes, you've reached the point where you decided to switch goals – from your career to your family – but perhaps you feel that something is missing?'
C. 'You're absolutely right. A man's a fool to keep struggling when nobody cares a damn. You did the right thing and I'd do the same in your position.'
D. 'As you have become older, you find more and more satisfaction with your family.'
E. 'Why do you feel that you weren't a success with the company? What do you mean by success?'

Statement 4 (from woman, aged 41): 'When I moved to the city I thought I'd build a bigger network and make lots of new colleagues and friends. I've always valued the social side of my job, and it's important for generating new ideas and maintaining my creativity … But, it doesn't seem to happen somehow. The work is fine, but there is not much time nor opportunity to socialise externally.'

Choose one of the following responses:
A. 'Can you tell me more about how you go about "networking"? Have you made any efforts recently to meet people?'
B. 'It sounds as though you may be a bit disappointed. Perhaps you were hoping that "networking" would happen more easily.'
C. 'Big cities are not friendly. Is that what you're saying?'
D. 'That sounds like a waste of opportunity. What you've got to do is get out and start "networking". If I were you I'd get started straight away.'
E. 'Well, let's see. There are lots of professional organizations in which you could get involved. Next month there's the annual forum and I could get you on to the guest list. What do you think about that?'

Statement 5 (from man, aged 32): 'I'm telling you, Lewis has really got his knife into me. I got the blame for the whole of the Brown and Williamson affair and there were eight of us involved. Now he's trying to insinuate that I'm falling down on the job. I had a good name in this office until he came here. He just doesn't like me and he's determined to get me down.'

Choose one of the following responses:
A. 'You are getting paranoid feelings about Lewis. Could it be that you are working out your frustrations at not getting the job you both applied for?'

B. 'You're right, he can really be a mean so-and-so when he chooses to, but I wouldn't go about it with your attitude.'

C. 'Have there been any other occasions when he's tried to show you up in a poor light?'

D. 'If I understand you correctly, you feel persecuted by Lewis and think that he intends to ruin your reputation.'

E. 'Right, you need to protect yourself from situations like this. Do you know that the union is becoming very strong amongst our grades? In fact, I've got some application forms here which I can help you to fill out.'

Scoring

The scoring grid is organised so that the situations (1–5) are identified in the vertical column on the left, while the response types are identified in the top horizontal row. Moving row by row, circle your response letter for each situation. Next, add up the total number of responses circled in each column and put the totals in the bottom row.

RESPONSES

	E	I	S	P	R
SITUATION 1	E	D	C	B	A
SITUATION 2	A	E	C	B	D
SITUATION 3	C	B	A	E	D
SITUATION 4	D	C	E	A	B
SITUATION 5	B	A	E	C	D
NUMBERS OF RESPONSES					

Figure 4.1

You should now have scores for all five types of responses. The total of your totals should add up to five.

E = Evaluative response (making judgements).

I = Interpretive response (reading between the lines, making hunches).

S = Supportive response (sympathy, agreeing, backing up, offering psychological and physical support).

P = Probing response (questioning, asking for more – often deeper–information).

R = Understanding/reflecting response (empathy, non-directive, non-evaluative response reflecting back to the speaker what was said).

Rogers' studies found that these five response categories accounted for 80 per cent of messages sent between people. Usage rankings were found to be: E – used most frequently, I – used next most, S – used third most, P – fourth most, R – used least.

In everyday conversation there is no right or wrong type of response. The appropriateness of different responses will depend on the situation. However, if you over- or under-use certain types of responses, then your conversational style may be annoying, or even offensive, to others.

When facilitating, the most appropriate and useful type of response is R, the understanding or reflective response (although the other responses will sometimes be necessary). If you did not score any Rs on the inventory, then you may need practice to get used to making this kind of response.

(Exercise adapted from Pedler, Burgoyne and Boydell, 1986
A Manager's Guide to Self-Development, McGraw-Hill)

If you tend to give reflective/understanding responses in day-to-day conversation you will find it easy to adapt to giving reflective responses when operating in a facilitative style. If you tend to give evaluative or probing responses, you may find it difficult to add reflecting to your repertoire of responses. Expect to be awkward, slow and hesitant at first. You will need to concentrate very hard in order to reflect accurately, and you will also need to think about how to rephrase what you have just heard. Keep practising because it *will* become easier, quicker and more natural in time. Incorporate it gradually into your style. You could try it out in safe environments (with friends and family) before trying it out at work. Practise reflecting initially in a role-play situation if it is very uncomfortable for you. Remember, if it seems difficult, it is because your mind is having to cope with a lot of things at once:

- Concentrated listening – what exactly are they communicating?
- Timing – when to respond.
- How much of what you have heard you should be reflecting.
- How much to interpret without overinterpreting.
- How to word your reflection without sounding like a parrot.
- Keeping track of your own train of thought throughout the process.

A few words of caution regarding reflecting. First, avoid starting all your reflective statements with the same few words. This is a frequent mistake at first. 'So, you ...' is the most common. Used too many times in a row, the same initial phrase sounds very repetitive and superficial. Vary your words as much as possible. Reflective responses can also be questions or statements. Here are some opening phrases which can be useful for reflecting and checking understanding:

- If I understand you correctly ...
- It seems as if you feel ...
- Do you feel ...
- What I am hearing is that you ...
- Am I correct in saying ...
- So, you think that ...

Second, compose your reflective statements carefully so that they are not leading, manipulating, or patronizing. For example, a reflective statement which overinterprets – 'So what you are *really* saying is ...' – can be very irritating. You do not want to mandate how the speaker is really feeling or what they are saying. Instead, you want to suggest how you think they might be feeling based on your interpretation of what they have communicated. So, 'Do you feel ...' is better than 'You must feel ...'

Third, try not to simply use phrases such as 'I understand, but ...', 'I hear what you are saying', or 'I know what you mean' – they are not truly reflective. These phrases may not convince people that they have been understood properly because you have not shown *what* you have understood them to say.

EXERCISE 11   Recognizing reflective responses

If you have completed the Typical Response Inventory (Exercise 10), you will have an indication of how you typically tend to respond to people in everyday conversation. This exercise gives you practice in recognizing an empathetic reflective response.

Pick out the response which best reflects what the subordinate is communicating; in other words, circle the response which demonstrates most empathy with and understanding of the subordinate's point of view. Also, try to identify which type of responses the other choices are. Compare your thoughts with the answers listed at the end of the chapter.

1. Subordinate: 'I'm getting nervous because June is coming. If I don't pass the Series 7 test, I won't be able to move into the position of stockbroker, which is my reason for joining this firm in the first place.'

Responses:
a. 'This upcoming test is making you anxious because there is a lot riding on it.'
b. 'Don't worry. You will be fine. Just keep your nose in the books.'
c. 'You should have more belief in your abilities.'
d. 'You worry far too much. The test is not so difficult. If you are worried now, you are going to have a hard time as a broker. It is stressful work.'
e. 'Are you behind in your studies?'

2. Subordinate: 'My supervisor is moving me into commercial sales now – just as I am beginning to excel in private sales. Will I never be allowed enough time to become successful in this organization?'

Responses:
a. 'You should be pleased. Commercial sales is a wonderful opportunity!'
b. 'Why don't you like commercial sales?'
c. 'You feel you are being moved before you are ready?'
d. 'The commercial sales department has a very good record. You will have as much opportunity there as you do in private sales, if not more.'

3. Subordinate: 'Ever since I've got out of the hospital after the car accident, I've felt fragile and insecure. I can understand my feeling that way when I have to drive, but I don't understand why I am feeling it at work. How long is this going to last? People are going to lose faith in my capabilities.'

Responses:

a. 'You are a strong person. It won't be long before you are back to normal.'
b. 'Have you talked to a doctor about this?'
c. 'People are seeing you as vulnerable, and treating you differently than they did before.'
d. 'Why don't we get together for a drink after work and see if we can cheer you up.'
e. 'You are concerned that your confidence in general seems to be shaken since your accident, and you wonder how much this will affect your work situation.'

EXERCISE 12   Generating reflective responses

Generate reflective comments in response to the statements below. Write your reflective responses on the lines below the statements. There is no one 'right' way to reflect but some suggestions are given at the end of the chapter.

1. Subordinate's statement to manager:

'I can't contribute much to those project meetings. There is nothing additional I can offer when both Mary and I are present because Mary knows more about our department's involvement with that project (sounding disappointed). The others must wonder why I even attend. But I need to hear firsthand what happens in the meetings. They make such a difference to my understanding of how our work fits into the bigger picture.'

_____

_____

_____

_____

2. Supervisor's statement to manager:

'I have been trying without success to get my staff to bring their own ideas to our weekly meetings. I've given them meeting agenda news beforehand so they can think ahead about the topics. I've told them time and time again that I want their involvement. But they clam up as soon as the meetings begin. I find myself having to do all the talking. It's like pulling teeth to get them to elaborate on responses to my questions and ideas.'

_____

_____

_____

_____

3. Account manager's statement to colleague:

'I would like to get my ideas acted upon. It doesn't matter whether I put forth my suggestions in writing as memos, or verbally in meetings, or even informally over lunch. Nothing ever comes of it.'

_____

_____

_____

_____

4. Employee's statement to personnel officer:

'This company is not what it claims to be! All this talk about caring and about developing staff. I am so overworked, and my manager never asks me to stay late – he just tells me! And, I still have not been able to attend that training course I was promised.'

_____

_____

_____

_____

5. Salesperson's statement to regional sales manager

'Since my wife left me I have been indifferent. I always worked so hard to support my family, and now my sales figures are slipping. I just don't seem to be very motivated.'

_____

_____

_____

_____

EXERCISE 13   Practising reflecting

You can practise responding with empathy in a role-play or in everyday conversations. If your score for R (reflecting/understanding response) on the Typical Response Inventory was two or higher, then practising reflecting probably will not be very difficult for you. But if you naturally tend to use a lot of evaluative or probing responses, then learning to use reflective responses might be awkward and difficult at first. For this reason, I suggest that you practise reflecting first in role-play situations, then practise during conversations at home or with friends, before trying it out on subordinates. At first you will be slow, hesitant, and you may lose your train of thought. Once you get used to it, though, you will see how beneficial reflecting is.

Remember to:

- Use 'you' or 'your' where they have used 'I', 'me', 'my'.
- Reflect feeling as well as content.
- It is often useful to reflect the feeling and then the reason for the feeling: 'You feel ... because ...'.
- You do not need to reflect everything they say. Try to reflect the main message(s) being communicated.

Summarizing

When facilitating, it is very useful to summarize at certain points during the conversation. Summarizing is different from reflecting. Reflecting is playing back what the person has communicated in their last statement or paragraph; summarizing is concisely listing and/or tying together the main points covered so far during the meeting/conversation, or during a major portion of the conversation.

Like reflecting, summarizing makes the person feel listened to and helps them to organize things in their minds. It also gives them an overview of what they have covered, and allows them the opportunity to assimilate and contemplate the discussion from a more detached perspective. This can help them to decide where to next direct the conversation.

They may throw a lot of confused talk at you, some related and some unrelated to their main concern. In these cases, you need to help them to sort out the issues. One way to do this is to summarize the issues which have been mentioned and then ask them which one(s) they think should be dealt with first. For example:

Subordinate: 'The new machinery that has been purchased does not have some of the necessary features that the old equipment had. I am the only person who has been trained properly to use it ... My newest operator doesn't seem to fit in with the team at all ... The busy season is coming soon and customers are really pushing us. I don't know what to tell them ... I don't have enough time for all this.'

Manager: 'You have brought up several problems: the capability of the new equipment we've purchased, the training of the users, managing your new operator, the busy season and customer requests, and your lack of time. What do you think needs to be addressed first?'

Summarizing will often help them to pull together their thoughts and proceed in a meaningful way, and can stimulate them to move on to the next step in the process: looking into the situation more deeply; recognizing repeating patterns in themselves; looking at the situation from a new perspective; or deciding on a goal or plan of action. Summarizing can also be used as a transitional method for moving the conversation on when you feel the need for some of your own input.

Manager: 'You've indicated concerns in several areas. First of all, your bookkeepers are making more mistakes than usual, you feel pressured by your colleagues, and you are tired and feeling physically unwell. I'd like to comment on ... because ...'

Another helpful time to summarize is when the speaker dries up. If they have gone blank, lost their train of thought, or become confused, a summary will help them to pull together their thoughts and proceed in a meaningful way.

It is essential to summarize at the end of the meeting. If the meeting is one of a series, then it is helpful to begin follow-up meetings by summarizing the last meeting. Summarizing intermittently throughout is also beneficial, especially at points where the speaker seems stuck and unsure how to move on.

VERBAL NON-LISTENING

Because encouraging, reflecting and summarizing are such powerful prompters, they are often all the response that is needed during the first phase of the process. Unfortunately, everyone has some conversational habits which are not at all encouraging and, although they are necessary in some cases, they need to be avoided when you are using facilitation techniques. These 'conversation stoppers' are things that we say in everyday conversation when we do *not* really want to listen to someone. Some are habits which we have adopted to protect ourselves from having to hear others. Others are simply comments which tend to cut off the conversation, rather than encouraging people to go into more depth.

In some work environments, these are the only types of responses that employees hear when they approach a manager with a concern. Staff who take the trouble to approach others for help are often the most motivated and responsible, and it is important that they should not be discouraged by receiving a conversation-stopping remark in return.

Managers who use such conversation-stopping devices are often not aware that what they are doing can be harmful. They may be missing signals that more help is called for, and they may even think that they *are* helping. These managers do not realize the potential negative effects of verbally brushing things under the carpet.

The following phrases are ways of communicating to people that we do not really want them to continue. They are not helpful when facilitating.

Leading/directing the conversation

Notice the difference between Manager 1's and Manager 2's responses in the exchanges overleaf:

Salesperson: 'I'm worried about my relationship with the clients.'

Manager 1:   'Which clients in particular concern you?'

Salesperson: 'Client X and Client Y are the ones I am most worried about.'

Manager 1:   'Why those two more than the others?'

Salesperson: 'Because they are the largest sales volume clients for our latest software package.'

Salesperson: 'I'm worried about my relationship with the clients.'

Manager 2:   'You are worried?'

Salesperson: 'Yes, I dread having to tell them about the bug I have discovered in the new software package. They won't be pleased.'

Manager 2:   'You are dreading their reaction to the news? What concerns you most?'

Salesperson: 'I'm not sure what is the best way to break the news to them.'

Manager 1 led the conversation too much and ended up going down the wrong track. Manager 2 reflected and asked open questions which encouraged the salesperson to talk about what was really of concern. In this way, Manager 2 was able to get to the bottom of the salesperson's problem, which was finding the best way to broach the subject of the bug with the clients. Reflecting and asking general open questions that encourage the speaker to lead is the way to avoid Manager 1's trap.

Blaming

It's your own fault, you know. You didn't support his last campaign. No wonder he won't cooperate with you on your new project.

If you think they *are* to blame, there is not much point in telling them in this accusatory manner. You are likely to get a defensive reaction. More effective ways of challenging behaviour will be discussed in the chapter on challenging and confronting.

'It's all in your head'

Telling people that a situation or problem exists only in their mind makes matters worse. Their reality is real for them and, although they may be imagining some things, there are probably good reasons why they have these imaginings and feelings. In phase 1, accept their reality as they see it. Then, when they seem ready for the challenging phase, you can consider together to what extent their problems are imagined or created by themselves.

Interrogating

Probing question after probing question can seem invasive and accusatory.

Playing 'psychiatrist'

You are a bit neurotic. This is why you are so obsessively perfectionist about these reports.

Managers generally do not have the psychological expertise to label people, and they will be resented for trying to do so. Putting up an expert front will create a barrier and can do more harm.

Twisting their words

Subordinate: 'I don't think this department is running well. The A and B departments are much better organized.'

Manager: 'So you're saying you don't want to work with us any more.'

Sarcasm

Cynical or sarcastic comments create blocks and are always inappropriate to an encouraging atmosphere. These remarks make others feel defensive, or as if they are being teased.

Cheering up/humouring

You'll be OK. Let's go and have a drink.

Hang in there. It'll pass with time.

Don't worry.

Statements like these attempt to gloss over the speaker's distress. They prematurely attempt to make the person feel better. Many people genuinely think they are helping when they do this, but they are not. Brushing aside negative feelings is the same as dismissing the problem.

Not accepting feelings or disallowing negative feelings

You shouldn't feel angry about it. You should be grateful.

Everyone goes through these sorts of things.

Advice giving

This is what you need to do...

In some cases this is a necessary response, but it will not help the person to learn how to solve their own problem(s). It prevents them from talking and working out their own solution, instead making them dependent on you.

Leading statements

Can't you see that...?

Don't you want to be promoted?

These kind of statements are leading questions. They are not encouraging an honest exploration; they are directives disguised as questions.

LISTENING BARRIERS

Be aware of what is going on in your own head while you are listening. The following are some barriers to listening to look out for.

Fear of listening too well

Are you afraid to really listen? Do you fear losing your own train of thought if you listen too well? Or, do you fear that your opinion will be changed by listening? You may worry that if you do not jump in to disagree you will be seen to be agreeing. All these fears are in reality unfounded. If you lose your train of thought, it will be temporary. If your opinion is changed, maybe their ideas are better. And there will always be time later on, after you have finished listening, to make it clear that you disagree.

Listening for what you want to hear

Poor listeners tend to hear what they want to hear rather than what is actually being said. This can have a disastrous effect on relationships with staff.

Personal limitations which affect interpretation

Your basic assumptions can affect what you hear. These assumptions are based on your personal experiences and memories, perceptions, values, biases, attitudes, expectations and feelings.

Emotional reactions

Sometimes people react strongly to certain words or phrases which happen to evoke emotional responses. This interferes with their ability to hear what is said after the emotive words.

Lack of self-awareness

Lack of awareness of your own feelings and struggles makes it difficult to listen to those of others.

Thinking ahead

Words are spoken at a rate of approximately 150 per minute, but the brain can process information about three times as fast. When facilitating it is inappropriate to use this spare thinking time for planning your own next words or thinking about something else, as you might during ordinary conversation.

Self-consciousness

If you are worried about how you appear or nervous about what you are going to say next, you will be distracted from listening.

EXERCISE 14   Listening self-awareness

This questionnaire has been devised in order to help you to understand yourself better as a listener. Self-understanding is an important factor in self-improvement. Answer the following questions as honestly as you can.

What makes me want to listen to someone?

_____

_____

_____

What makes me feel good about the person I am listening to?

_____

_____

_____

What makes me feel negatively towards them?

_____

_____

_____

What do people do that makes me feel comfortable when listening to them?

_____

_____

_____

What do people do that makes me respect them when I am listening to them?

_____

_____

_____

What do they do that loses my respect?

_____

_____

_____

What things do people do that distract me when I am listening to them?

_____

_____

_____

What mannerisms do I find annoying when listening?

_____

_____

_____

What makes me lose interest in a person who is speaking?

_____

_____

_____

What subjects arouse strong emotions within me?

_____

_____

_____

What topics of discussion do I feel uncomfortable listening to?

_____

_____

_____

Am I often in a hurry when listening?

_____

_____

_____

Am I mentally overloaded most of the time?

_____

_____

_____

Am I distracted by what is going on around me?

_____

_____

_____

Do I feel self-conscious when listening?

_____

_____

_____

Am I often thinking about what I am going to say next?

_____

_____

_____

Do I often think that I already know what the speaker is going to say ahead of time?

_____

_____

_____

Am I often tired when listening? Do I use listening time to rest?

_____

_____

_____

Am I often confused by the topic or the speaker?

_____

_____

_____

Do I often daydream while listening?

_____

_____

_____

Do I worry about other things while listening?

_____

_____

_____

What do I tend to think about when I am listening to someone?

_____

_____

_____

What listening problems do I have?

_____

_____

_____

How could I be a better listener?

_____

_____

_____

SUMMARY OF LISTENING TIPS

- Stop talking. Give yourself the space and the time to really attend.
- Concentrate. Focus on what is happening and try not to be distracted.
- Check for understanding frequently by reflecting.
- Watch their body language.
- Listen to *how* things are said.
- Listen for what is *not* said – what is being avoided.
- Recognize your responses and try to put your own feelings aside. Are you switching off? Mentally arguing? Over-identifying? Stereotyping?
- Be aware of your own body language (SOLER):
    — Sit squarely
    — Open gestures
    — Lean slightly forward
    — Eye contact
    — Relax.

EXERCISE 11   Answers

1. a. Empathetic, reflective.
   b. Patronizing, dismissive of emotions.
   c. Directive, patronizing, judgmental.
   d. Judgmental.
   e. Probing.

2. a. Judgmental, dismissive.
   b. Probing, over-interpretation.
   c. Empathetic, reflective.
   d. Dismissive, leading, evaluative.

3. a. Evaluative.
   b. Probing.
   c. Over-interpretive.
   d. Dismissive, trivializing.
   e. Empathetic, reflective.

EXERCISE 12   Reflections

1. 'You feel in a bind because although you don't want to appear 'useless' at the meetings, you are in need of the information you gain from them. Is that right?'
2. 'So now you feel frustrated because your efforts to get more staff involvement in your meetings have not made a difference?'
3. 'You have contributed ideas which have not been acted upon. You seem frustrated/fed up/angry.' (Depending on the associated body language any of these feelings could be construed.)
4. 'You feel angry because you think that the company is all talk, no action, when it comes to concern for its employees. Is that so?'
5. 'You have become complacent about work since your wife left. Maybe it seems your motivation for working has lessened or disappeared.'

5

Questioning Techniques

There are many purposes for asking questions. Different types of questions will be used in varying frequencies depending on which phase of facilitation you are in. Some reasons for asking questions are listed below.

THE PURPOSE OF QUESTIONS

- Demonstrating interest. Asking an appropriate and intelligent question is a way of showing that you are listening.
- Clarifying. Clarifying questions help to clear up any confusion, giving you a clearer view of the big picture.
- Probing. A focusing question encourages elaboration on areas you think may be significant for the speaker.
- Checking facts. This type of question should only be asked when necessary in order to have a clear understanding of the situation. Don't divert the conversation with unnecessary fact-checking.
- Eliciting personal reactions. At work people tend to speak on a logical level, leaving out emotions. Questions regarding feelings will give permission to talk on an emotional level.
- Testing interpretations, understanding, and conclusions. A reflective question asks whether your interpretation of what they have said is accurate.
- Challenging. Questioning is the most useful form of challenging.
- Making suggestions. Questioning is a subtle way of putting forward your own suggestions (ie without being too directive).

It is not appropriate to ask questions simply out of curiosity. Satisfying our curiosity may be tempting, but it won't help to create an atmosphere conducive to opening up and solving problems/taking on challenges. If the questions are not leading in a direction which will help the person to look into or resolve the situation, they may pick up on this and feel uncomfortable.

TYPES OF QUESTIONS

Open questions

Open questions elicit a long response or explanation. They are useful for getting people talking, probing, eliciting personal reactions, challenging and making suggestions. These questions often start with words or phrases such as 'How', 'Tell me about', 'Why' and 'What'. Examples of open questions are, 'Why do you think that is so?', 'How did you deal with the situation?' and 'What alternatives do you have?'

Responses to open questions tell you more about the respondent than response to closed questions, because open questions do not place limitations on or lead the response. Note the difference between the open and closed questions below.

Closed: 'Did you think yesterday's conference was successful?'

Open: 'What did you think of yesterday's conference?'

The closed question is likely to invoke a 'yes' or 'no' as an answer. From this you learn, for example, whether or not they thought the conference was effective, but you do not learn about the thinking or reasoning behind their answer. The second question is more likely to elicit a response which explains *why* they thought the meeting was effective or not. The response to the second question is also more likely to tell you what is important to this particular person. They might mention the politics of the meeting, whether it ran over time, or whether or not a conclusion was reached.

Closed questions

Closed questions – questions which have yes/no answers or simple, quick answers – such as 'Did you attend the plant safety training course?', 'How many years have you been in this position?' or 'Which department do you work in?' tend to generate short answers. Closed questions are useful for clarifying or for checking facts and for getting people to be more precise and specific in what they are saying.

Some people have a habit of asking many closed questions, and they often do not understand why they have difficulty getting and keeping conversations going. People often ask closed questions which would get a more useful response if they were asked as open questions, as illustrated in the examples below.

Table 5.1 Open questions/Closed questions

Closed questions	Open questions
Did your promotion improve your situation?	How has your promotion affected you?
Have you talked to your staff about the project results?	How did you handle your staff regarding the project results?
Are you excited about it?	How do you feel about it?
Do you approve of the way the programme is being run?	What do you think about the way the programme is being run?

Probing questions

Probing questions are questions leading on from or going deeper into what the person has previously said. They can be either open or closed. A probing question or remark invites them to discuss an issue more fully. Here are some examples:

Closed question:	'Do you like the new telephone system?'
Response:	'No.'
Open question:	'Tell me about the problems that you are having.'
Response:	'It is more trouble than the old system we had. Everyone is struggling with using it. It is questionable whether the investment will pay off.'
Probing/open question:	'Why do you think people are finding it difficult to use?'
Probing/closed question:	'Would you struggle less if you received more training on it?'

Probing questions are useful for obtaining more details, clarifying, eliciting feelings, comprehending the thinking behind actions and encouraging elaboration on issues brought up tentatively. Only ask probing questions if they are relevant to the situation. Do not ask them just for the sake of filling up a space in the conversation. Silence is much better than a useless question.

Continuous probing sounds interrogational and can direct the conversation too much. Probing needs to be interspersed with empathetic responses and open questions which do not direct the conversation, but instead allow time and space for the person to lead the discussion and to go deeper into the 'real' issue. Notice the difference between the managers' responses below.

Subordinate: 'I'm afraid I won't be able to handle this new position.'

Manager 1:   'Which bit can't you handle?'

Subordinate: 'It's the demanding clients.'

Manager 1:   'Which clients are demanding?'

Subordinate: 'The M&G Company and BDZ Ltd are the most difficult.'

Manager 1:   'Why are they difficult?'

These are very common responses in everyday communication. But look what happens when more empathy and less directive questions are used:

Subordinate: 'I'm afraid I won't be able to handle this new position.'

Manager 2:   'Can you tell me a bit more about your fears?'

Subordinate: 'Some of the clients are demanding. When I get pressured by them, I become ineffective.'

Manager 2:   'Do you feel you can't cope under pressure?'

Subordinate: 'I just lose my ability to think straight when I am pushed or harried by others.'

Manager 2:   'So you are having difficulty concentrating when clients pressure you?'

Subordinate: 'Yes. I don't know if there is anything I can do about this.'

It is important to move forward slowly and carefully. Do not jump in too quickly. Wait to let the full picture emerge before focusing the conversation. When probing, be careful about using 'Why?'. It can sound critical.

EXERCISE 15   Question types

This is an exercise to help you to determine which question types you naturally tend to use more or less of.

You need two people to work with you: one to converse with, and one to record the kinds of questions you use in the designated chart below.

The chart is designed so that the recorder can record the types of questions used in the chronological order in which they are asked by making ticks, moving left to right over the time period covered (five–ten minutes is suggested). When a probing question is asked, the recorder will need to tick twice to designate whether the probing question is open or closed. See examples below.

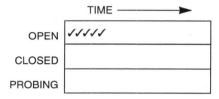

Figure 5.1 Example of someone who asks many open questions

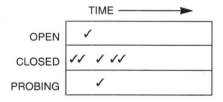

Figure 5.2 Someone who asks many closed questions

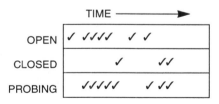

Figure 5.3 Someone who asks many probing questions

Pick a topic which is conducive to asking questions – perhaps their job, or their last holiday. Ask the person who will be talking with you to answer only the questions which they are asked.

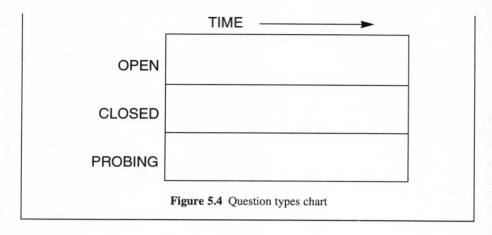

Figure 5.4 Question types chart

Leading questions

Leading questions are best avoided in most business situations, and particularly when facilitating. They steer the other person to answer in a particular way.

There are two ways of asking leading questions. One is by tagging on a leading phrase such as 'isn't it', 'don't you', 'haven't we' on to the beginning or end of your statements: 'This is a wonderful book, isn't it?' or 'Don't you think this is a wonderful book?'. The other is by stating your own or someone else's opinion first, and then asking the other for theirs: 'I think this is a wonderful book. What do you think?'. People may answer leading questions unaware that they are being led in their response; or they may be aware of what's going on and feel annoyed about being led.

To summarize the risks inherent in asking questions:

- Too many questions might make it feel like an interrogation.
- Questioning might put the manager in control of the conversation, not the 'subordinate'.
- Employees might get too used to this conversational style and stop talking spontaneously, instead waiting for questions from the manager.

6

Challenging and Confrontation

Facilitating is not only about listening, accepting and showing empathy. It also means helping people recognize and change less effective patterns of thinking and behaviour. The aim of challenging or confronting established patterns is to expand the person's awareness in some area. We want to help them to either:

- Consider other ways of *interpreting* things, or
- Discover different ways of *dealing* with things.

An example of a distorted perception which can be challenged through facilitation is over- or underrating oneself, while an example of unproductive coping behaviour which could be tackled is isolating oneself from colleagues. In the second example, the subordinate's perception of the situation (racist attitudes and comments, for example) may be accurate, but isolation from one's colleagues is not the most productive way of coping.

For many people, challenging is the most difficult part of facilitating others' development. It involves an element of risk because the other person may react negatively to the challenge. Negative reactions to challenges are often due to oversensitivity to criticism, pride, or difficulty in admitting faults, especially if the view or behaviour pattern has been held for a long time, or you are dealing with a martyr-type personality who enjoys complaining more than changing. Also, people are likely to feel more comfortable with you when you are in empathetic mode than in challenging mode and they may try to convert you back. Challenging people is difficult, but when it is successful it speeds progress towards developing action plans, so do not be discouraged.

WHEN TO CHALLENGE

Timing is very important. Confronting should occur *after* the first phase of relationship development has been established and the situation has been defined *as the employee sees it*. They need to have 'unloaded', expressed their emotions and begun to feel trust in you. Your challenge is much more likely to be listened to and considered once you have listened to and shown empathy with them, once they feel accepted and understood. You need to have gained a full understanding of the situation before you think about challenging it. One clear indicator that they are ready to be challenged is that they start to challenge themselves: questioning their own point of view, or constructively analyzing, evaluating, and criticizing themselves. In the example below the subordinate suddenly queries whether his or her own behaviour is contributing to the situation.

Subordinate: '...I just don't understand! How could he continue behaving this way? Why won't he be honest and discuss things rationally? I can't count on anything he says any more. Maybe it's something I'm doing, although I can't think what!'

There are exceptions to the above rule about waiting for the appropriate time to challenge. In certain circumstances challenging will need to happen earlier in the process, for example:

- When the person's behaviours are causing great distress to others.
- When the person is very hostile towards you.
- When the person's behaviour is adversely affecting the unit's productivity.
- When the person's behaviour is self-defeating.
- When there is time pressure to improve the situation.

Where these circumstances apply, the situation should be explained to the employee.

Keep in mind that there may be other factors which make it inappropriate to challenge – perhaps you are feeling impatient or in the mood for a fight, or the employee is feeling particularly emotional or vulnerable.

WHAT TO CHALLENGE

The following is a list of some of the circumstances in which challenging may enhance progress:

Discrepancies between verbal, vocal and body messages

As discussed earlier, challenging can be helpful when confusing or conflicting messages are being communicated.

Example: Michael *says* everything is going well, but his fists are clenched, his body tense and his words short and sharp.

Incongruities between words and actions

An employee's actions may not conform with what they say.

Example: Joan says she is interested in and committed to the ABC project, but she does not turn up at the project planning meetings.

Incongruities between past and present remarks

Sometimes, attitudes expressed in the present contradict attitudes which have been expressed in the past.

Example: Simon says he finds his committee ineffective, whereas before he emphasised how productive the group was.

He may have changed his mind, he may be ambivalent, or one or the other of the statements could have been hiding his real attitude. Challenging will help you find out what's really going on.

Unrealistic self-image

Often, people under- or over-rate themselves, or are unaware of how they appear to others. When your own and others' experience of the person differ significantly from their image of themselves, challenging is a way of pointing out that their perception of themselves does not match up with your own or that of others.

Waffling or rambling

Going off at tangents, talking in circles, over-elaborating on trivial details, not talking about the real issues or not making sense are all warning signs that communication is less than effective. An indication that someone is waffling is when you start to get confused or bored. The chances are that they are not talking incisively enough.

CASE EXAMPLE 3

A senior manager from a national health organization came to me for coaching to improve his management skills. When I asked what in particular he wanted to work on, he proceeded to describe how wonderful his job was, how important he was within his company and how well furnished and decorated his office was. He told me about the politics within his organization, his achievements and his reading in the field of psychology. He name-dropped many famous psychologists and business management gurus. He talked very loudly and quickly for about ten minutes, and did not make much sense.

By the end of all this I was a bit dumbfounded. I repeated my question: 'So, what aspects of your management skills do you feel you need to work on?'. He then began to explain that he was well liked as a manager, and had been cheered wildly by his employees during a skit he performed at a company party. I asked again, 'Which parts of your job do you find difficult?'. He gave me an explanation of how to use fishbone diagrams and mind maps when running a meeting. I asked again, 'What did you come here to work on?'. He looked down and said quietly, 'I suppose I tend to be too dominant'.

This is a simple (and somewhat amusing) example. This person went from being extremely indirect and protective to being direct, concise and honest, just by my repeatedly asking the question in different ways. Often it takes considerably more time and effort than this, especially when the person has well-developed defence mechanisms. And people can be quite skilled in their efforts to confuse or mislead you regarding the true nature of the problem, even when a part of them really would like to open up.

Misinformation/misperceptions

People sometimes give inaccurate information or leave things out. They generalize and exaggerate. Encourage them to take a more objective view of the situation. People may need to be reminded about points they have forgotten or overlooked. Their point of view may be keeping them locked into their situation, or even creating their problems.

Overlooked alternatives

People are sometimes reluctant to acknowledge that there are courses of action other than the one they have chosen. Encourage them to think and talk about what *they* can do in the future rather than about what others might do to them. People often need help in order to realize that their own action or inaction is contributing to a situation for which they are holding others entirely responsible. If they say there is *nothing* they can do to improve the situation, urge them to analyse whether this is really the case or whether they are simply *unwilling* to do something different. If they *could* be doing something different, they need to look into why they aren't or why they don't want to.

Preoccupation with the past – or the future

This can often be to the detriment of the present.

Self-destructive beliefs

'Should', 'ought' or 'must' beliefs are taught to us as children by our parents, our religion or by society. Sometimes they are traditional beliefs which have been passed down without much thought having been given to them. People often feel guilty if they do not go along with these 'rules'. If they do go along with them, they feel annoyed about being compelled to 'follow the rules' when they do not really want to. They may not realize that they have a choice in the matter. For example, consider the rule: 'One must not be rude'. There is a time and place for saying what you think even if it might be considered rude. Someone who rigidly adheres to this belief may be unable to say what they mean, which could cause them great difficulty. Challenging people whose 'shoulds', 'oughts' and 'musts' are getting in their way will help awaken their awareness of what is happening, explore what their beliefs are (and these will often be subconscious), where they come from, and the effects they are having.

Irrational beliefs

People sometimes have unrealistic or unfair beliefs which, although they may not be operating at a conscious level, can make life very difficult for them and those they work with. Table 6.1 lists some common irrational beliefs and some alternative rational beliefs which employees can be encouraged to adopt instead.

Self-destructive behaviour

Not recognizing or considering the consequences of their behaviour can have an alienating effect on others. Encourage them to explore their behaviours in order to understand them better and to change them if necessary. Look into the motivations and meanings behind behaviours.

Example: Bill is competent in his work but irritates others, both senior and junior to him, with his excessive and sometimes flippant use of humour.

Table 6.1 Irrational belief/Rational alternative

Irrational belief	Rational alternative
I must never make mistakes.	The only way not to make mistakes is to do nothing. I'm active, and all active people make mistakes.
Other people should not make mistakes.	No one is perfect. I can accept that other people will make mistakes.
Other people make me angry.	I make myself angry when I don't accept that other people don't live up to my expectations.
Other people should live up to my expectations.	Other people don't need to live up to my expectations.
My happiness depends on other people's behaviour and attitudes.	My happiness comes from within me and does not depend on others.
I must live up to other people's expectations.	I don't need to live up to other people's expectations to be OK.
I must win.	According to the law of averages most people only win 50 per cent of the time. I don't need to win to feel OK.
Life should be fair and just.	Life is not fair and just.
I must get my own way.	I do not need to get my own way to feel OK, and can sometimes get satisfaction out of letting other people have their own way.
I need other people's approval to feel OK.	It is nice to get others' approval, but I do not need their approval to feel OK.
I must always please other people.	It is unrealistic to expect that I can always please other people.
I must never get angry.	It is OK to be angry sometimes.
I can't be happy if people misjudge me.	People sometimes misjudge me. That is inevitable. But I know that I am OK and that is what matters.

Source: Geldard (1993)

Stuck in a behavioural rut

General passiveness, being a martyr, overoptimism, overpessimism, being a victim or always blaming others may mean that employees are inadvertently contributing to a problem which they themselves are attributing to external forces.

> Example: Susan is overworked. She blames others for giving her too much to do and for taking advantage of her helpful nature. She resents being 'the responsible one' and sees the others as irresponsible. Yet at the same time, she seems to take pride in being so needed/important.

Refusal to see other points of view

This can be for any number of reasons: arrogance; attachment to traditional working methods; bad experiences in the past. Challenging can help overcome entrenched attitudes.

Reluctance to act on intentions

Making resolutions is one thing; acting on them is quite another. This is why following-up is so crucial.

Topics/facts avoided

Look out for relevant things which they *do not* talk about. They are deliberately avoiding a basic issue which seems to be bothering them.

Feeling abnormal

People often worry that their feelings are not normal. Distress can often be greatly reduced if they can begin to understand that their feelings are a perfectly normal response to the situation. People worry that they are crazy for having certain feelings, and often feel very guilty about having negative feelings: for example, they might feel angry with a member of staff for being ill and thereby increasing their workload. The charts of stages (life stages, transition stages) provided in Part IV are useful for understanding emotional reactions. It is very important for managers to understand these emotional responses, as well as the behavioural responses which result from them.

Repeated themes in conversation/recognized behavioural patterns

By listening to employees talk and considering how different parts of their dialogue have similarities or could somehow be related, you can give feedback on recurring themes or patterns which they may be unaware of.

WAYS TO CHALLENGE

There are two basic methods of challenging: pushing and pulling. These are the fundamental categories of influencing. Pushing means being directive: telling, demanding, explaining your reasoning. Pulling is facilitative challenging through questioning. Pulling is slower and gentler, but usually more effective, creating greater commitment to change on the part of the employee. In most cases it is best to challenge by pulling first, resorting to pushing only when pulling is not working quickly enough.

Pushing may inhibit the individual rather than encouraging them to open up. They may become defensive, angry, withdrawn, rebellious or upset. If they are submissive, pushing can make them more dependent on your opinions rather than more independent. However, there are a few people who can handle pushing and actually prefer it to the pulling approach. These people have strong egos and prefer that you 'tell it to them straight'. You need to know the person you are working with in order to assess how well they can cope with direct challenge. If they can handle it, the push approach is quicker. If you are going to push, do it clearly and concisely. If what you are saying is your own interpretation or someone else's opinion, then acknowledge that. It *is* appropriate to push when you are simply correcting misinformation.

Because the pulling approach encourages self-challenging and self-criticism, it engenders more self-responsibility, self-confidence and greater commitment to change. Pulling takes the form of asking questions and making suggestions tentatively and carefully. In the example below, Manager 1 makes a pushing challenge, whereas Manager 2 makes a pulling challenge:

Manager 1:   'Other people don't see it that way. They think that you are taking too much risk. People are reluctant to approach you now.'

Manager 2:   'How do you think the others view your behaviour?'

Instead of *telling* them what other people think try *asking* them to imagine how another person might see the situation. If, after the manager has tried the pulling approach, the subordinate cannot conceive how others are thinking, the manager can always use the pushing method.

If you choose the pushing method, be careful how you word it. Manager 1 below is too harsh. Manager 2 pushes in a more respectful manner, and Manager 3 pulls.

Manager 1: 'It's your own fault, you know. You ignored or dismissed everything he said during the discussions we had. No wonder he won't cooperate with you on the project.'

Manager 2: 'I think he might be behaving uncooperatively because he feels you are ignoring him. He seems to be disappointed when he is not responded to. What do you think?'

Manager 3: 'Why do you think he doesn't want to cooperate? Could there be any reason why he is uncooperative?

CASE EXAMPLE 4

George worked in a computer firm and had been given an opportunity to move from his present position as a programmer to work at a more senior level as a trainer. He was apprehensive about the new job, never having worked with people much before. He was concerned that he was meant to be a 'techie' and that he didn't have the right personality for training.

As I spoke with him, he came across as a thoughtful, warm person, with an ability to listen and a lively sense of humour. I predicted that, given some facilitative counselling and coaching, he could become a very competent trainer. But there was also the possibility that George simply had no interest in training. I did not share any of my thoughts with him initially. Instead, I took him through a line of questioning in order to understand him, and to challenge his thinking.

George: 'I am not the man for the job.'

Me: 'What would the right man be like?'

George: 'Articulate, confident and good at understanding people.'

Me: 'How articulate do you think you are?'

George: 'Well, I can explain things well enough to individuals when they come to ask me questions, but I don't know how to manage a whole group of people all at the same time.'

Me: 'Is managing a group of people an inborn or a learned skill?'

George: 'I suppose people do learn it, but probably some are naturally better at it than others. I don't think I will be good at it.'

Me: 'And if you don't think that you have this natural ability, what makes you think that?'

George: 'I am much better at working by myself with things than with people.'

Me: 'Why do you have the idea that you don't work as well with people?'

George: 'I don't know. I just don't feel right. I don't feel I belong in a training position.'

Me: 'What could be the reasons for your feeling you don't belong in a training position?'

George: (*getting impatient*)
          'I don't know! It's just how I think based on what I know of myself!'

Me: 'Well, for example, could your feelings be natural nervousness regarding doing something new, or have you encountered bad experiences managing groups of people, or do you not like the idea of training, or has someone in your past told you that you are better with machines than people, or can you think of any other possible reasons?'

George: 'No, it is just how I understand myself.'

Me: 'Why do you think you were chosen for this position?'

George: (silence) 'Well, I suppose people do tend to come to me with questions. I am just uncomfortable about the idea of being a trainer. Maybe it is just apprehension, but I don't know.'

Me: 'Do you think you might enjoy training if you learned the skills needed?', etc.

There are, of course, many ways of challenging the same situation. Here are some examples:

Misinformation/misperception

Sometimes people tend to see things in a pessimistic way. We can't simply dismiss their negative feelings because there is in all probability a valid reason why they see things negatively. So, simply telling them not to be pessimistic won't help. But, through skilful challenging with questions, you can sometimes help them to change the way they perceive events and situations. You can help them to look at things more objectively by questioning them about positive aspects of the situation, or you can ask them if they can come up with more constructive ways of dealing with the situation.

Subordinate: 'My newest member of staff, John, is continuously in and out of my office. He is asking me to help him with things he could easily resolve for himself. He knows how busy I am. Quite frankly, John has become a bit of a pest, taking up too much of my time. It has got to the point now where I am quite irritable when I speak to him.'

Manager (pulling):
'I can understand that this must be a nuisance when you are so busy. What do you think is going on in John's mind?'

If the subordinate cannot think of any positive ideas, the manager can then put forward a positive interpretation in the form of a question:

Manager: 'It seems that your input is very important to John. Is it possible he may be wanting to get to know you a bit better or to communicate with you a bit more?'

The manager has offered an alternative interpretation of John's behaviour. Instead of seeing it as a negative nuisance, it can be regarded in a positive way in that John, being a fairly recent addition to the staff, may be trying to build up a relationship with his boss, and that this just happens to be at a time when the boss is very busy. Maybe John simply feels neglected. The manager's interpretation could be wrong, however, which is why it is important to put forward interpretations tentatively. It could be that John is a perfectionist and anxious not to make any mistakes.

Discrepancies between verbal, vocal and body messages

Manager: 'You say you are fine, but I see you looking tired and sounding down. Your voice seems lower and quieter than normal.'

Incongruity between words and actions

Manager: 'You have said that you are not overworked in your new position, but I am a bit confused because I've noticed that you frequently look rushed or harried, and that you are staying in the office much longer than usual in the evenings.'

Unrealistic self-image

Manager: 'You describe yourself as really struggling with managing project teams, yet I see you as being quite competent in this area and I think my colleagues see you as being competent as well. Why do you think there is this discrepancy in our views?' or, 'Do you think you may be expecting too much of yourself?'

Waffling and rambling

You need to take action to focus the conversation. This can be done by pointing out what you have noticed is happening and asking them to point out what is significant. Ask them what is important, and get them to focus on those aspects of the situation.

Manager: 'It seems that the conversation is digressing from what is most important to you, and I am aware that we only have 35 minutes left.'

When someone talks in a general sense and is not specific enough for you to really understand the crux of the situation, you may need to ask for more precise information. For example:

Subordinate: 'I can never get through to Michael.'

Manager: 'In what specific ways do you find it difficult to get through to him?'

Subordinate: 'Michael never understands me. He misinterprets my comments and actions. He responds to something other than what I mean to say.'

Other phrases you could use to encourage specifics include: 'Explain to me what you mean by ...' and 'Can you give me an example of ... '

Overlooked alternatives

Manager: 'Do you see any similarities between the predicament that you are in and situations that others have been in? What might others have done to improve such a situation?'

CASE EXAMPLE 5

Judy had been the manager of a nursing home within a large private medical organization for six years. During her first four years in this position, she had performed extremely well and had continuously maintained both the highest profit figures and the highest customer satisfaction survey results. However, during the last two years her figures had begun to slip, and recently her figures and results had dipped below average levels.

Judy's regional manager, Robert, had not had much success in finding out the specific reasons why Judy's performance had deteriorated, even after having repeated conversations with her and having surveyed all the staff in the home. Judy said that there was not a problem and the figures were going down due to the 'nature of the market nowadays'. However, other nursing home managers were not in the same situation. Robert called me in as an external consultant to have a series of confidential conversations with Judy.

I chose to initiate the process in 'push' mode. Judy needed to do something about the situation. I firmly explained to her that at this point, when the company was paying for expensive external consultancy, she could no longer not do anything as the company would take further action if she herself did not.

Once I had shaken her into reality, and into the immediacy of the need to take action, I 'pulled' to get her to open up about what was going on. This led to her admission to losing interest in nursing home management. She was bored and wanted to work three days a week to lessen her boredom. I questioned whether this was practical or possible and she said that, as a single mother, she needed her income and that the role did not lend itself to part-time work. I used 'pulling' questions to find out what work she would enjoy more. She suggested hospice care, expressing an interest in the psychology of the dying and their family members. I again used 'pulling' questions to get her to consider her realistic options. She considered the pros and cons of going to work for a different organization and of finding a different position within the same organization, possibly creating a new role for herself if the right one did not exist. I asked her to consider how she might continue to explore the possibilities on her own. This resulted in her deciding to follow two paths simultaneously, exploring hospice work in other organizations, while seeking the help of Robert in exploring hospice work possibilities within her own company.

Self-destructive beliefs

Supervisor: 'I just can't figure out a fairer way to divide up the sales territories. No matter what I do someone will be unhappy and I will be seen as unfair.'

Manager: 'You seem to think that you must make life 100 per cent fair for your sales team. Do you think that this is possible?'

Stuck in a behavioural rut (panic, in this example)

Subordinate: 'I am terrified of speaking to everyone at the next board meeting. I am flattered to have been asked to present the plan for the telecommunications project I've been working on, but the thought of getting up in front of all those people who can affect my future is giving me grey hairs.'

Manager (*after* reflecting feelings and getting subordinate to discuss them thoroughly):

'So you are very apprehensive about the board presentation, especially since you feel it is so important to your career. Could you possibly think of your nervous anxiety as nervous excitement – excitement about an opportunity to shine and impress everyone?'

Reluctance to act on intentions

Manager: 'You keep mentioning that you would like to develop yourself further and to move beyond your research position into consultancy. Have you taken any action to start moving yourself towards the consultant's position?'

Repeated themes in conversation/recognized behavioural patterns

Manager: 'You have talked about three areas which are troubling you: not having enough contact with your subordinates to keep on top of things, being unable to monitor the accuracy of the packaging and shipping department when they send out your products, and being unable to get HR to assist you the way you want them to. All three of these problems involve control. It seems as if lack of control is an issue for you at the moment.'

TIPS FOR FACILITATIVE CHALLENGING

It is not a good idea to suddenly change from being empathetic to being completely confrontational. Challenging needs to be approached slowly and bit by bit. Mix in empathetic responses with your challenges and they are likely to be much better received. A useful approach is to reflect what the person has said and then immediately follow it with a challenge. The reflection reassures them that they have been heard and understood, before you go on to offer a different perception. If you give advice which consists of statements like, 'If I were you ...', then you are not facilitating – you are talking down to them.

When you need to give feedback, either your own opinion or others', do not treat those opinions as being statements of fact. Using 'I' statements rather than 'you' statements helps to establish them as opinions. For example, saying 'I found your report difficult to follow because the order of the topics did not make sense to me' will be better received than a statement like, 'Your writing does not make sense because you didn't put the topics in a logical order'. Even worse would be a statement like 'You are not a logical writer', which makes a judgement about the person rather than the behaviour. This sort of statement is very likely to get a negative reaction.

A statement of your feelings can be useful too. The statement, 'I am a bit confused' (in the example given above for challenging incongruity between words and actions) softens the challenge because it raises a query rather than stating an opinion.

Sometimes a simple summary of what the employee has said will help them to see if they are being unfair, one-sided or biased. They may respond by bringing up someone else's point of view, or suggest another way of looking at things.

Manager: 'Are you saying that your department needs exclusive access to the Mac equipment?'

Subordinate: 'Well, I suppose the other departments need to use it sometimes. It's just that we use it more than any other department, and we usually need it at short notice. Perhaps it would be better if we bought new machines especially for our department.'

When adopting a facilitative style, you should allow for the possibility that you will be confronted by them as well as vice versa. This can be used as an opportunity for you to set an example of how to think about and respond to challenges and confrontations. Talk about your own and others' experiences only as a last resort and even then only tentatively, making sure to acknowledge that the situations are not necessarily exactly the same.

In general, is very important to challenge tentatively when you are unsure of whether the challenge is correct or not. You do not want to hold back from challenging for fear of upsetting the person, but if you can learn to put forward your challenges carefully, you can raise issues and considerations whilst minimizing the risk of the person becoming defensive. Too much challenging can be discouraging, so proceed with caution. Unless the case is particularly serious, leave the ultimate 'diagnosis' of the situation and the decision-making responsibility up to the employee.

EXERCISE 16   Challenging

When was the last time someone presented you with the circumstances listed below. What could you have said to challenge the person in the most constructive way? Assume for the sake of this exercise that rapport and empathy have already been established. Write out your challenges in the spaces below the statements.

Waffling or rambling

_____

_____

_____

_____

Misinformation/misperceptions

_____

_____

_____

_____

Incongruities between words and actions

_____

_____

_____

_____

Incongruities between past and present remarks

_____

_____

_____

_____

_____

Irrational beliefs

_____

_____

_____

_____

_____

Unrealistic self-image

_____

_____

_____

_____

_____

Discrepancies between verbal, vocal and body messages

_____

_____

_____

_____

_____

Overlooked alternatives

_____

_____

_____

_____

_____

7

Facilitating Problem Solving/Management

There are many books on the process of problem-solving. You may prefer to work through a specific model of your own. This section will cover the general concepts of which you need to be aware in order to help people with problem management.

The basic steps in problem-solving/management include:

- General goal.
- Specific objectives.
- Objectives prioritization.
- Strategy for action.
- Monitoring of implementation.

GENERAL GOAL

In order to increase the chance of your staff putting the necessary time and effort into executing the problem-solving steps, it is important that they take full responsibility for managing the problem and commit themselves to their goal. You need to make sure they are convinced that the goal is both beneficial and achievable, and are willing to put the necessary effort into working towards it. The goals and the action steps need to feel as if they are their own, not someone else's.

In order to help an employee to determine their goal, it is useful to ask them: 1) What alternatives exist?; 2) How could things be different?; or 3) What would they like to be able to do differently? Negative definitions of problems can be turned into positive goals. For example, 'Stop overreacting and being irritable with staff' can be translated into 'Managing difficult staff situations calmly and rationally'.

The goal is likely to be a very general one, such as 'Become more effective in meetings' or 'Be a better supervisor'. The next step is to break the goal down into objectives which are specific enough to work with.

SPECIFIC OBJECTIVES

Objectives need to be clear and specific enough to apply action plans to. In order to help turn a goal into more precise objectives, we can ask questions such as:

What would the current problem "look like" if it were better?

What would you be doing that you are not doing now?

What would you stop doing that you are doing now?

(Egan, 1990)

Are new behaviours going to be added? Are old behaviours going to be reduced? Is a new behaviour going to replace an old behaviour? For example, a supervisor's objectives might be to keep his/her temper, to script feedback before meeting with staff, and to make an effort to improve his/her communication with the department's secretaries.

Objectives need to be realistic and achievable, otherwise people will become discouraged. Sometimes they will be attempting to change very long-term habits. It is a good idea to apply realistic time-limits to the objectives in order to both motivate and avoid eternal procrastination. In other words, the objectives should include an approximate time horizon stating when the objective will be achieved by: next month? next quarter?

OBJECTIVE PRIORITIZATION

Next, the objectives need to be prioritized. People cannot do everything at once, and they will become demotivated if they try.

They could prioritize in order of importance. Or you might suggest that they prioritize the objectives based on which, when addressed, will affect more than one area of their work (ie start with the one which will have most far-reaching effects). It is not necessarily a good idea to start with the most severe problem – that might need to be worked up to. Limitations imposed by their schedule might also make one order of priorities more practical than another.

STRATEGY FOR ACTION

The employee now needs to formulate an action plan which will enable them to achieve their objectives. Work with the objectives, one at a time, in order of priority. You will need to help them to think about how to go about achieving each objective in turn – to consider and choose from the different strategy options available.

It is very important that they do consider a range of alternative action plans for achieving the goal, and that the implications of these are contemplated carefully before action is taken. This means helping them to avoid the temptation to jump in and run with the first idea that comes to mind. Their plan needs to fit in with their overall lifestyle, goals, and values. It needs to make sense, be practical, and the timing must be realistic.

The following types of questions will help to stimulate employees' imaginations and encourage them to come up with creative ways of achieving their goals (Egan, 1990):

- How? How can you get where you would like to go? How many different ways are there to accomplish what you want to accomplish?
- Who? Who can help you to achieve your goal? Who are the people who can serve as resources for the accomplishment of this goal?
- What? What resources – both internal and external – are needed for you to accomplish your goals?
- When? What kind of timing would be best for you to achieve your goal? Is one time better than another?

Once you have tried to get the employee to come up with their own ideas, you may want to put forward some suggestions of your own. The way that these suggestions are put forward is very important. A good approach is to put ideas forward in the form of questions: 'What do you think about doing X?'; 'How do you feel about Y idea?'; 'Could you do X?'; 'What would happen if ...?'; 'What are the pros and cons of doing A?' This last question is helpful because it puts the onus on the *employee* to consider both positives and negatives, and therefore seems more neutral.

Along with action plans, ways of monitoring progress need to be planned at this stage. Methods of monitoring are discussed in the following section.

MONITORING OF IMPLEMENTATION

The employee needs to decide how they will monitor their efforts and progress. If their action plans fail, they need to focus on what can be learned from the experience. If circumstances change, they need to be encouraged not to give up, but to adjust the action plan accordingly.

The provision of motivators and support is vital in order to inspire action. People need to keep themselves motivated by giving themselves regular incentives. Small rewards after each little bit of progress is made generally work better than one large reward obtained once the overall goal has been achieved. People should reward themselves for taking action, irrespective of whether the desired results ensue!

Ideally, the rewards should be small things which they enjoy, but which they would not normally allow or do for themselves. If the rewards are too expensive, they won't be able to reward themselves frequently enough, and if the rewards are things they are getting now, they will not be novel enough to act as an incentive. Things like bouquets of flowers, luxury food items and magazines make good rewards.

In addition, support from others is invaluable to someone who is trying to make changes. Suggest that they find reliable sources of support to call upon, such as a colleague, the company training or personnel department, their partner or a support group.

Once the skills of problem management (from identifying the problem to setting goals to taking action) have been learned, employees can then implement the process independently in other areas of their work. Here is an example of how the problem-solving process might work:

General goal

Having expressed dissatisfaction about problematic situations with his boss, his colleagues and his partner, the subordinate defines his problem generally as relationship difficulties. His goal is, therefore, to improve his relationships.

Breaking the problem down into its constituent parts

Having been probed by his manager to think about what might be causing those relationship difficulties, the subordinate comes up with the following:

- Impatience and irritability.

- Bitterness from those he was promoted over.
- Failure to listen to others.
- Procrastination in dealing with things.
- Not enough time in the day.

Determining specific objectives

The manager then asks the subordinate what he thinks he should do differently in order to improve his relationships. The subordinate comes up with:

- Be more calm and controlled.
- Become a better listener.
- Improve time management.

Prioritizing objectives

The manager then asks the subordinate to consider which of these three takes priority. The subordinate prioritizes the goals in the following order:

- Become a better listener.
- Be more calm and controlled.
- Improve time management.

Determining concrete steps to achieve goal 1

The manager asks the subordinate to think about the steps that need to be taken in order to become a better listener. The subordinate says:

- Read some books about listening.
- Try to listen more during conversations.

The manager wants to make some of the steps more concrete: 'Try to listen more during conversations' is a bit vague. How could you tell when this had been achieved? The manager asks the subordinate, 'When exactly, where, how, and with whom do you plan to do this? How will you monitor yourself?' The subordinate then rewrites the steps as:

- Ask a communications consultant for a recommended reading list on listening.
- Pick two books from the list and read them while travelling to visit clients.

- Listen more than speak during the first half of my regular Monday morning meeting with my boss.
- After each meeting make a note of how well I am able to achieve this.
- After four meetings ask my boss whether she has noticed a difference.

Take first action step(s)

The subordinate goes off and puts the plan into action.

Review progress and reward self for taking action

At a later date the manager inquires about progress. The subordinate reports that, although he has a long way to go to becoming a 'good' listener, he has begun to make some progress. The books he has read have given him some very useful tips. He has kept records on his meetings with his boss, and knows that he has been listening for a higher percentage of the time than he used to. Unfortunately, his boss has not noticed the difference. The manager reminds the subordinate that, regardless of others' appreciation or lack of it, he must reward himself for his achievements in whatever small but meaningful way he can. The subordinate buys himself chocolates on the way home from work on days when he has made significant efforts.

Review overall plan

The subordinate decides that the plan is working well so far. He will find two more areas in his life where he can systematically apply and monitor his listening skills. The manager asks the subordinate how he might apply a similar problem-solving process in order to achieve the objective of 'being more calm and controlled'.

8

Facilitating Decision-making

Decisions are difficult because they are usually not black and white. Pros and cons must be weighed, making decision-making frustrating, confusing, and possibly even frightening, rather than cut and dried. When there will be losses no matter which option is chosen, people may resist making a decision. However, once people are aware of this and come to accept that loss is inevitable no matter what, it will become easier to make the decision. If you work through decision-making with the employee in a facilitative style using one of the processes below, they will have a tool which will make them more self-reliant when it comes to future decision-making.

FORCEFIELD ANALYSIS

One useful device to introduce to someone struggling with decision-making is forcefield analysis. Forcefield analysis is helpful when making a simple decision such as whether or not to take a particular action. The process involves considering and weighing the forces operating for and against the particular action.

For example, Chris is trying to decide whether to buy a new brand of software package for the department or stick with the one they are already using. Looking at the decision to buy the software, the forces for and against are listed on opposite sides.

Table 8.1 Buying new software

Forces for	Forces against
Faster speed of processing	Expense of purchase
Extra customized data fields	Time and cost of retraining staff
Easier to make inquiries into system	Will need to change entry forms which other departments use
0800 software support service	

The forces are then ranked for importance (one to ten, one to five...) and the totals for each side calculated.

Table 8.2 Buying new software

Forces for		Forces against	
Faster speed of processing	3	Expense of purchase	7
Extra customized data fields	6	Time and cost of retraining staff	9
Easier to make inquiries into system	5	Will need to change entry forms which	
0800 software support service	2	other departments use	2
Forces for	**+16**	**Forces against**	**-18**

It is important to recognize that a decision should not be made based solely on the resulting numbers. A higher total for forces acting against buying the new software package in the above example does not necessarily make not buying it the appropriate decision. One needs to reconsider the weightings and check for omitted forces. Forcefield analysis is a tool which aids thinking about decisions in a systematic manner, displaying the pros and cons in a manner which is easy to review. It does not necessarily provide the definitive answer. Remember that the pros and cons for various parties need to be considered: for the company and its goals and for other people/departments as well as for the individual him/herself.

Decision-making becomes more complex when there are several alternatives to be considered. Possible questions to consider when comparing alternatives include:

- Which option seems most workable?
- Which solution has the best chance of success?
- How expensive is each possible solution?
- How much time will each solution involve?
- How risky is each possible solution?
- Which solution can everyone decide to fully commit to?

(Pokras, 1989)

Pokras also suggests useful processes for comparing alternatives, such as the consequences worksheet and the criteria matrix.

CONSEQUENCES WORKSHEET

A consequences worksheet helps people to compare whether the potential benefits and rewards of certain actions/solutions justify the potential costs and risks. Benefits and rewards are considered relative to personal performance plans and departmental and organizational objectives. Potential costs and risks can be assessed by predicting ramifications.

Solution	Potential costs	Potential risks	Possible benefits	Possible rewards	Conclusions

Figure 8.1 Consequences worksheet   *Source:* Pokras (1989)

CRITERIA MATRIX

A criteria matrix is an organized and quantifiable method for visualizing alternatives. Alternative solutions are listed vertically in the left column and the criteria to measure them are listed horizontally across the top. Ratings go inside the grid, and total ratings for the solutions go in the last column (on the right).

Alternative solutions	Evaluation criteria					Total rating

Figure 8.2 Criteria matrix   *Source:* Adapted from Pokras (1989)

Ratings can vary in their complexity. You could use a +, −, or ? scale; an A,B,C scale; or a numerical scale (1 to 3, 1 to 10 ...)

Alternative solutions	Evaluation criteria					Total rating
	Accuracy	Cost	Morale	Confident-iality		
Hire full-time staff	5	1	4	5		15
Hire part-time staff	5	3	4	4		16
Hire temporary staff	2	4	2	1		9

Figure 8.3 Simple criteria matrix

Once again, the ratings will need to be reconsidered for congruity once the grid is completed. The grid's result is only as accurate as the individual scores.

When working with someone on decision-making, if possible do not push too quickly for a decision then and there. Leave them to their own devices. Sometimes people just need time to think.

9

Other Elements of Facilitative Coaching/Counselling

MEETING STRUCTURE

Opening

As a manager there will be many times when you *do* take the lead and assume a position of authority, and your staff may expect that from you. So it is all the more important to establish that this time the discussion is going to operate in a facilitative style and therefore will be a meeting of equals. Do this early on by setting up the room appropriately, displaying listening responses and by encouraging the person to take responsibility for helping themselves. When they enter the room, greet them warmly using their Christian name, and offer them a seat. Then say something which makes them feel welcome and acknowledged.

Here are some examples of appropriate openers:

- 'Good morning, Jill. Please have a seat. How can I help you?'
- 'Good morning, Jill. What is on your mind?'
- 'Good morning, Jill. I understand you want to talk about ...'
- 'Good morning, Jill. Tell me about the situation.'

If you, rather than the employee, have initiated the conversation, then be upfront about why you have arranged the meeting:

'I am aware that you have not briefed your team about the new production system. I was wondering if anything is going on. I've got some time if you would like to talk.'

It is important not to seem rushed, yet clear time boundaries need to be set at the start, along with limitations on confidentiality (if appropriate). If the meeting is only going to be partially facilitative, it is a good idea to say which parts will be so, and which parts will be otherwise.

Physical set-up

The room set-up and seating arrangement can greatly contribute to or detract from creating the right environment. Both communicate your attitudes in a subtle but significant way.

Chairs placed at a slight angle to one another generally make people much more comfortable than chairs placed straight across from one another. Sitting directly opposite someone (Illustration A), it is easy to feel confrontational. Sitting at a 90 degree angle (Illustration B) is better but not ideal because this angle can make it difficult to make eye contact. Sitting at an angle slightly off head on (Illustration C) is the ideal arrangement for facilitation. This way it is easy to observe the other person and make direct eye contact, but equally easy to break eye contact at times when it is appropriate.

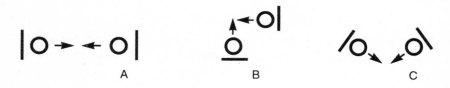

Figure 9.1

It is best to use either no table or a low coffee table so that physical barriers are kept to a minimum, and body language can be observed. If a table is necessary for papers and writing, then a small round table is more flexible than a square or rectangular table or desk because there is a range of possible angles at which you can place the chairs. If you must use a table with sides then sit at right angles on one corner rather than straight across from one another, and turn the chairs slightly towards one another. Comfortable soft chairs are a nice touch, but if they are too low and soft they are not conducive to creating a serious atmosphere.

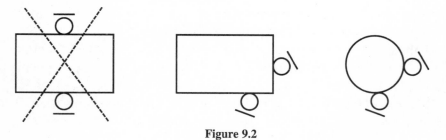

Figure 9.2

The room to be used should be thought about ahead of time. Rather than meeting in either of your offices, a neutral meeting room, such as a small conference room, will help avoid distractions and remove power differentials.

Closing

You will need to prepare the person for the end of the meeting. About ten minutes before time is due to run out, tell them how much time is left. It is useful for them to be aware of the limitation on remaining time so that they can decide how they want to use it. They may want to go into an area you have not yet covered, or to go further into an area previously only touched upon.

Then, two or three minutes from the end, summarize the main points covered during the meeting. If you plan to meet again, arrange the time and summarize the action to be taken by either of you before the next meeting. If you will not be meeting again, then leave them with some positive feedback or something constructive to think about. Here is an example of how this might work.

Area manager to retail store manager:

> I see we're running out of time. Let's see if we can pull together what we've covered. You began by explaining why you are becoming dissatisfied in your current position as you approach retirement age. You feel more and more removed from your staff, in terms of both age and style, and you would like to move to the IT department at central office, where you can make use of your favourite hobby and pastime, computing, during your last five years. You are aware that this has only been a whim up until now, but you are feeling more and more discontented as time goes on. During the course of our conversation, you have determined that it is time to do something. Maybe between now and next time we meet you could do some networking as you suggested, in order to see if your skills could be used in that department.

KEEPING THE FOCUS

When someone is focusing excessively on another person (or people), it is important to redirect the conversation towards their focusing on themselves, and taking responsibility for their own actions. Often people will talk about situations, especially difficulties, in the third person: 'He said..., she said..., he did..., she did...' Valuable time will be wasted if the focus is not kept on the person in front of you and his/her own actions, thinking and feelings. Discussing others overextensively is not going to help them to decide what action to take for themselves.

Subordinate: 'My assistant has been frequently absent recently. He is going through a divorce, and I think he is finding it very stressful. I am finding it difficult to cope without him, especially since his absences are sporadic and unpredictable.'

Manager 1:   'So your assistant is going through a difficult divorce...'

Subordinate: 'My assistant has been frequently absent recently. He is going through a divorce, and I think he is finding it very stressful. I am finding it difficult to cope without him, especially since his absences are sporadic and unpredictable.'

Manager 2:   'You are frustrated because you don't know when he will be out of the office.'

Manager 2 managed to keep the focus on the subordinate, whereas Manager 1 was directing the conversation towards externals – the assistant, the difficult divorce.

Encourage them to focus on themselves by using 'I' statements rather than outwardly-focused 'he', 'she' or 'they' statements. This will encourage acknowledgement of their feelings, thoughts, and actions and ownership of their own issues.

Focusing on externals is very common, especially since those who come to us often really believe that the problem belongs to another person and not to them. There is nothing wrong with the question that Manager 1 asks in the example below. It is simply inefficient use of time to consider someone else's point of view when the employee's own point of view has not been examined fully. In the beginning the focus is best kept on the employee themselves. Once you have fully explored the problem as it exists for them *and* explored their feelings about it *and* are ready to move on to changing the way they perceive and deal with the problem, then this question would be appropriate.

Subordinate: 'My secretary is continuously irritable. She is difficult every time I ask her to do something.'

Manager 1:   'Why do you think she is irritable?'

Subordinate: 'Maybe she's having difficulties at home. She is irritable with other people as well.'

Subordinate: 'My secretary is continuously irritable. She is difficult every time I ask her to do something.'

Manager 2: 'What effect is this having on you?'

Subordinate: 'It's making me avoid her.'

Manager 2: 'You now prefer not to have contact with her?'

Subordinate: 'Yes, and this is now affecting our work!'

Manager 2's response focuses on the subordinate and the effect the situation is having on him/her. Talking in this way will help the subordinate to see that the situation *is* causing a problem for him/her and that action needs to be taken on his/her part to attempt to remedy it.

Not only do we want to encourage people to acknowledge ownership of a situation, we may also need to take this a stage further and encourage them to acknowledge that their own action (or inaction) may be supporting or perpetuating some things, and/or preventing other things from happening.

SYMPTOM OR CAUSE?

Be aware that an original problem as first presented is often not a full explanation of the real problem. It could be a symptom of the underlying problem or it could be totally unrelated, especially if the person feels too uncomfortable to jump straight into talking about the real problem. Sometimes a smaller 'sub-problem', part of the bigger, deeper problem, is brought up. Be aware that this occurs and be prepared to either probe, or to offer plenty of space (silence) to let things emerge in order to be sure of having a full picture of the situation before moving on to problem-solving. They are likely to need encouragement to delve deeper.

Probing carefully will also help to determine the best method of problem-solving for the particular situation. It is all too easy to send someone who is struggling on a training course which sounds as if it will cover the general area of the problem. This is a common approach to problem-solving. If the training does not address the real issues, however, it can be an expensive error. Using facilitation techniques can sometimes be more effective (and cost-effective) than a training course. At other times the person's problem may be part of a larger organizational problem. Try to uncover and tackle the real issues underlying superficial problems.

CASE EXAMPLE 6

Susan was a young applications administrator within a large insurance firm. She had been with the company in this position for eight months and her supervisor, David, was concerned because she was not performing as well as he had expected her to. She did not seem to remember procedures and was always asking himself and other colleagues for help with simple tasks. David was puzzled because the work was not difficult, and Susan had performed well during her induction training.

When David met with Susan to chat about how things were going, she expressed no concern about or dissatisfaction with her performance. When David mentioned that she seemed to need a lot of help, Susan said that she tended to be a bit forgetful, but that people were always very helpful.

David, annoyed by her frequent requests for help, was tempted to say that he was very concerned about whether Susan was the right person for a role which required efficiency and organization and that she needed to pull her socks up. Instead, he asked her whether she thought she was happy in the position. She responded that she was, but that she would prefer to have an assistant to help her. David questioned Susan at length regarding why she should need an assistant when no one in that position before had ever needed one but was getting nowhere until Susan finally gave an emotional reason instead of trying to rationalize: 'I suppose it would just be nicer to have someone to work with and talk to.' David asked whether she had ever worked alone before and it turned out that her previous jobs had all been very social. Susan then realized and admitted that she deliberately forgot how to do things so that she would have an excuse to go and talk to people.

David's patient and determined questioning got to the underlying problem (loneliness) behind the surface problem (ineffectiveness). He and Susan could then work together to decide how best to manage the real problem (the cause), rather than focusing superficially on a single result (symptom) of that problem.

INTERPRETING/OVERINTERPRETATION

Overinterpreting, or interpreting too quickly are common mistakes when we first begin to listen actively and respond to others.

Reading between the lines and following hunches can usually only be carried out successfully by experienced psychologists. You should only interpret *very* tentatively, putting forth your interpretation as a question, and only when there are definite indicators (body language, tone of voice) as supporting evidence.

The following is an illustration of the consequences of interpreting too quickly, and therefore focusing on the wrong topic:

Security department head:

> 'Our security system is extremely out of date. I can't get the guy in charge of purchasing to understand me. He's hopeless! The cost of investing in a new one is a lot less than the cost of theft. People go unchecked in and out of this building as they please.'

Manager: 'So we are having a problem with theft then.'

The real concern of the security head may well be the unsatisfactory nature of communication with the purchasing department and the process for making purchasing decisions, or it may be a conflict of personalities with the 'guy in charge of purchasing'. This manager assumed that theft was the most important issue because he or she jumped to conclusions too soon. More open questions (which don't lead the conversation) and/or listening are essential at this stage in order to discover which issue is of real concern to the security department head.

Here is a situation where the manager is overinterpreting:

Regional sales manager:

> 'One member of my sales team, Jill, is cleverer than I am. She often wants to rewrite bits of my proposals.'

Product manager:

> 'You feel threatened by Jill's intelligence.'

Unless there had been previous indications, or telling body language or tone of voice were displayed along with the sales manager's statement, this would be overinterpretation. The sales manager did not mention feeling threatened. Maybe he or she feels proud of Jill and her intelligence, and excited about what she can contribute to the sales team.

Your interpretation may or may not be correct. The person you are talking to might have a completely different and legitimate interpretation or explanation. Therefore, interpretations should be put forward very tentatively, allowing the employee plenty of opportunity to modify them. If the sales manager in the last example sounded angry and was physically tense, then a better response might be:

Product manager:

> 'You seem a bit anxious. Is something about this worrying you?'

If the sales manager's voice or body language gave no indication regarding the nature of his feelings about Jill's cleverness, then asking a simple question such as 'How do you feel about that?' would be more appropriate.

SILENCE IS GOLDEN

If facilitation skills are used appropriately, there will be silent periods in the conversation. At first, this might make you uncomfortable. Many people are uncomfortable with silence and feel as if they need to fill it by saying something. When facilitating, however, silence actually improves the conversation dramatically. It allows both parties time to consider what has been said, to gather thoughts and clarify them. Silence also gives time and space for the parties to get in touch with thoughts and feelings which are not so immediate and close to the surface. If you talk too much, you block the other person from thinking, feeling and talking. Using silence effectively is another way of encouraging them to take responsibility for talking about the real issues. This silent time is not wasted; on the contrary, it is very productive.

The employee's silence could mean any one of many things: sorting out thoughts; feeling emotion; wanting you to speak; conveying anger; refusal to engage; not having words to express their feelings; blockage or blankness; respect; fear; boredom; or sadness. If they are silent for a very long time, try talking to them about what the silence means.

EMOTION

In order to facilitate development effectively, you need to understand emotions. When people bring problems to you, there are two ways in which emotions can have an effect on the conversation. First, they might be in an emotional state to start with, or suddenly have an emotional outburst during the course of the conversation. Second, they might be repressing their emotions in a detrimental way. In the first case, you need to know how to respond to their emotional behaviour, and in the second case you need to identify and encourage the expression of the repressed emotions.

Outbursts and ventilation

When someone is in an emotional state, you need to be aware that they will need a period of time to discharge the emotions (in Phase 1) before moving on to either define or resolve the problem. You need to allow this discharge, often referred to by psychologists as ventilation, to happen. You might even see it as being a positive thing: discharging emotion will allow them to move on. Encouraging them to accept and express their emotions (for a reasonable period of time) is important. If emotions are not dealt with, feelings will often bubble beneath the surface and have a detrimental effect, perhaps blocking him/her from proceeding, or manifesting themselves as unwanted behaviours.

In British society, people are ashamed to show emotion. Managers tend to think that they are doing the proper and polite thing by ignoring emotions; that they are behaving in a professional manner and helping people who might be embarrassed about a display of emotion to save face. However well-intentioned, this attitude can cause a lot of damage because it can mean situations are not fully worked through and resolved. Time and time again I have seen delegates on my courses practise facilitation in role-plays and make the mistake of ignoring emotions even when they have been clearly verbally expressed. When these delegates stuck to logical, matter-of-fact problem-solving and did not acknowledge or demonstrate understanding of the feelings communicated, 'subordinates' continued to express their feelings, sometimes verbally, at other times non-verbally, preventing the process from continuing until they were acknowledged.

How should you deal with strong emotions? Allow people to cry or to be angry for a while. Give them an appropriate period of emotional ventilation. Acknowledge verbally what they are feeling. This is likely to be what is needed in order for them to move on.

The same is true of other emotions, such as anger. So long as they are not threatening to you or to company property, allow them to express their anger. While they are expressing strong emotions you may feel at a loss as to what to do. The best thing to do is as little as possible. Anything you try to discuss while they are in a highly emotional state will not be heard anyway. Just wait patiently. The only useful comments are reflections of what they are feeling, and reassurances that their feelings are normal and natural, which show them that you understand and accept their emotions.

After they have had a chance to express their emotions, their mind may be clearer, their will and confidence stronger, and they are more likely to be ready to resolve matters on their own. At other times, seeing them through an initial emotional phase will lead to their being able to begin expressing their thoughts in a rational enough manner to begin determining specifically what the problem is and what can be done about it.

Repression

The diagram below shows the interaction between feelings (emotions), thoughts, and behaviours.

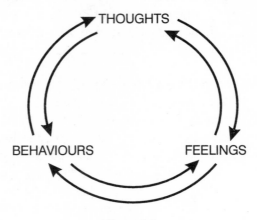

Figure 9.3

The inner arrow demonstrates the cycle in one direction: feelings affect thoughts which affect behaviours. Thoughts are often expressions of feelings at various levels of awareness. If someone is exhibiting strange or inexplicable behaviours, it may be due to a repressed feeling. For example, belligerent behaviour towards authority figures could be due to a fear of them. The person may not be aware of the feeling (fear), and may not even be conscious of the resulting behaviour (belligerence). One example might be a supervisor's compulsive perfectionism which causes him/her to continually watch over employees' shoulders. The underlying feeling could be inadequacy. Feelings are often displaced on to a safer and easier target. For example, anger towards a dominating partner could be taken out on staff. Once the feeling is revealed, acknowledged, expressed and accepted, then the behaviour is likely to lessen. Unexpressed feeling often lies behind poor performance.

When people avoid discussing emotions – refusing to acknowledge emotions and talking only on a logical level – and you suspect there are indeed emotions involved, encourage them to talk about the repressed feelings. You could choose either to reflect only the emotional content of their communication, or ask direct questions about what they are feeling.

Positive thinking

The emotions/thoughts/behaviours cycle works in both directions. The outer cycle of arrows illustrates that thoughts also affect feelings, which in turn manifest themselves in behaviours. This cycle in the diagram is very useful for explaining to people the power of positive thinking. Changing their thoughts can help people feel more positive. Note that positive thinking tends to work only *after* negative feelings have been validated; otherwise, it just becomes another way of repressing them.

Emotional blocks to taking action

Emotional blocks can stop people from taking action even when, on a logical level, they want to do so. If there is no apparent reason why someone is not implementing their action plan, then there is likely to be an emotional block which is preventing them from doing so. Try to help them to recognize and work through the block.

Ask them about the thoughts and feelings which may be blocking them. For example, you could ask, 'What are you feeling when you consider doing X?', or 'What thoughts are going through your mind when you imagine trying this option?' Becoming aware of and talking about the blocks will help them to overcome them.

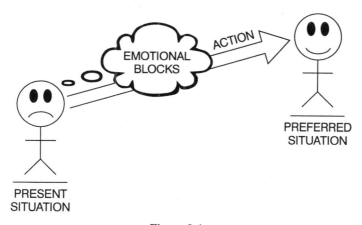

Figure 9.4

Some common emotional blocks which impede taking the action necessary in order to bring about desired change include:

- Fear of failure or of their efforts being wasted.
- Fear of other people's reactions to their changes.
- Fear of higher expectations from other people and/or not being able to cope with new situations.

- Uncertainty about choice: 'Am I making the right decision?'
- Difficulty visualizing self in new position.
- Fear of unknowns and risk – the present situation, however unsatisfactory, is comfortable because it is predictable. The change itself can be what is frightening them. People are creatures of habit: they get used to being unhappy, and the fear of change (which leads to a new, unknown situation) can be greater than the fear of remaining unhappy in the present situation. And if they do begin the process of change, frightening new feelings can result.

REFERRAL

A manager who is proficient in facilitating development will tend to attract people to come to him/her to talk. Inevitably, he or she will run into situations where it is not appropriate to help directly. Instead, the employee needs to be referred elsewhere. How do you decide when to refer? *Always* refer when you feel you are in over your head: when the situation is such that you do not feel qualified to help; you feel uncomfortable in doing so; or you do not have the resources at your disposal. You also need to refer when time constraints do not allow you to help. Do *not* try to take on everything yourself. If you do not refer when you are out of your depth, you could make matters worse. If you encounter a situation where phase 1 and 2 (developing the trust required for openness and defining the problem) are going to take a long time, it is likely that the person would be better off referred to a human resources professional or an external counsellor.

A SUGGESTION

Do not try to become proficient at all of the facilitation skills at once. You will be setting yourself up for discouragement and failure. Focus on one skill at a time. Wait until one feels natural, comfortable and effective before moving on to the next. You are likely to get *worse* before you get better, but keep going: you will improve. There are four stages which people go through when working on their interpersonal skills:

1. Unconsciously incompetent – you are blissfully unaware of your lack of skill.
2. Consciously incompetent – you receive some feedback, read a book, take a course, begin to realize that you can improve your skills.

3. Consciously competent – you self-consciously struggle to apply what you have learned. Things get worse for a while before they get better.
4. Unconsciously competent – as your new skills become more automatic, they become part of your natural style.

Moving through from stage 2 to stage 3 is the most difficult transition, but don't give up!

PART IV

Be a Manager who 'Spots the Opportunities'

Part IV has been included to provide you with additional information which will be useful when facilitating others' development (see Chapter 10 on human states) and to give you ideas regarding situations where facilitation can be particularly effective (see Chapters 11 and 12). Each of these topics is the subject of many books and the sections are by no means intended to be complete instructional material. Instead, they are intended to stimulate your thoughts with regard to applying the techniques.

10

Human States

It is often very useful to have a working knowledge of the most common human 'states', in order to help someone understand what is happening to them. People feel tremendous relief on discovering that their reactions are normal, and this knowledge will help them deal more effectively with their emotions and, subsequently, to move forward.

LIFE STAGES

People go through life stages in both their careers and their personal lives. Decisions and changes in both these areas will affect one another. You cannot assist employees with their career progression without taking the personal context within which those changes are made into account. It is crucial to understand the stages that people tend to move through, and to recognize major transition and decision points.

The following are some useful charts to refer to when helping staff put their personal and career development issues into some sort of perspective. The first focuses on adult personal development while the second is a chart of typical career stages and concerns.

Table 10.1 Major adult development periods

Age	Stage	Psychological issues
17–22	Early adult transition	Reducing dependency on parental support
		Exploring the possibilities of the adult world
		Testing out preliminary identities and life choices

continued overleaf

Table 10.1 *continued*

Age	Stage	Psychological issues
22–28	Early adult establishment	Making initial choices and commitments to occupation, relationships and lifestyle
		Initial development of life goals
		Establishing relationship with mentor
28–33	Age 30 transition	Working on limitations and flaws of first choices
		Challenging parental assumptions about life and career
		Making important new career/life choices or reaffirming old ones
33–38	Settling down	Building a niche in the world (work, family, community, friendships, interests)
		Defining personal direction and advancement
		Becoming own person
38–42	Mid-life transition	Taking stock of life so far
		Coming to terms with own mortality
		Developing stronger sense of who you are and what you want
42–50	Entering middle adulthood	Making crucial choices about who you want to be and what you want to do
		Taking more realistic world view
50–65	Age 50 transition to late adult transition	Re-evaluating what you have to offer life
		Achieving adult, social and civic responsibility
		Adjusting to retirement

Source: CEPEC (1992)

Table 10.2 Career stages and career concerns

Age	Career stage	Career tasks	Psychological issues
15–22	Pre-career: exploration	Finding the right career	Discovering one's own needs and interests
		Getting the appropriate education	Developing a realistic self-assessment of one's abilities
20–30	Early career: trial	Getting a viable first job	Overcoming the insecurity of inexperience; developing self-confidence
		Adjusting to daily work routines and supervisors	

Age	Career stage	Career tasks	Psychological issues
20–30 (*cont*)			Learning to get along with others in a work setting
30–38	Early career: establishment	Choosing a special area of competence Becoming an independent contributor to the organization	Deciding on level of professional and organizational commitment Dealing with feelings of failure of first independent projects or challenges
38–45	Middle career: transition	Reassessing one's true career abilities, talents, and interests Withdrawing from one's own mentor and preparing to become a mentor to others	Reassessing one's progress relative to one's ambitions Resolving work life/personal life conflicts
45–55	Middle career: growth	Being a mentor Taking on more responsibilities of general management	Dealing with the competitiveness and aggression of younger persons on the fast track in the organization Learning to substitute wisdom-based experience for immediate technical skills
55–62	Late career: maintenance	Making strategic decisions about the future of the business Becoming concerned with the broader role of the organization in civic and political arenas	Becoming primarily concerned with the organization's welfare rather than one's own career Handling highly political or important decisions without becoming emotionally upset
62–70	Late career: withdrawal	Selecting and developing key staff for future leadership roles Accepting reduced levels of power and responsibility	Finding new sources of life satisfaction outside of job Maintaining a sense of self-worth without a job

Source: Feldman (1988)

CASE EXAMPLE 7

Tim was 45 and worked as a mid-level manager within a large conglomerate. He had worked for this company for 23 years, steadily progressing upwards, and was comfortably established and well-respected there. He had recently received a promotion to a position two levels higher, which was going to offer him a lot more responsibility, though in a different section of the organization. When Tim received notice of his promotion, he was elated and very proud that his service and loyalty was paying off. He excitedly told all his family and friends the news. He was due to begin work in his new role in a month's time.

As the time to start work in his new role approached, however, Tim became more and more apprehensive. He decided to visit his boss, Carol, who, although sorry to lose him, was very pleased for him. Carol was able to see Tim immediately and invited him into her office. He explained how worried he was feeling about moving to the new role. Carol questioned him about his fears and was surprised when Tim talked more about his personal life than about the new role. He said he thought that his wife was not particularly thrilled about his promotion though she had not said so directly. But he was not clear about exactly what was bothering him. Carol suggested that they meet again in a week to talk more.

During the course of the next discussion it came to light that Tim had really been looking forward to taking it easier at work now, and to putting more energy into his hobbies, particularly gardening, a hobby he shared with his wife. He had only been partially aware that he was being more and more drawn to interests outside work, but became more conscious of this when the excitement regarding his promotion began to be replaced with a feeling of unease. Tim's ambitions were changing, and the promotion opportunity had made him realize this, and think about how he wanted to focus his energies in the future. He said that he would prefer to stay in his present position and hoped that the company would be happy to have him do so.

LIFE SKILLS

There are basic skills which are necessary in life. When people are struggling, it is often because they are either unskilled or neglecting their skills in a certain area. Areas where staff may need improvement include:

- Time management.
- Thinking processes.
- Relationships.
- Managing feelings.
- Education/learning.
- Relaxation/leisure.
- Health.

TRANSITION STAGES

When people go through a major transition, especially one which has been suddenly thrust upon them rather than chosen and anticipated (like redundancy or the death of someone close) certain feelings are commonly experienced, often in the order shown below (Kubler-Ross, 1975). The 'transition curve' has also been related to people's reactions to change in organizations undergoing major change initiatives.

1. Immobilization: a sense of being overwhelmed, frozen, unable to make plans.
2. Minimization: trivializing the change or disruption, denying the magnitude of its effects.
3. Depression: realities of the change become apparent. Feelings of powerlessness, and loss of control – especially of one's emotions – as depression sets in.
4. Accepting reality: process of unhooking from the past and preparing to face the future. Letting go of the past is important. Becoming more optimistic.
5. Testing: beginning to test out the new situation – trying new behaviours, life styles, and new ways of coping. Will probably be fragile – angry and easily irritated.
6. Search for meaning: following the testing period, concern with understanding the changes, seeking meaning for how things are different and why they are different.
7. Internalization: integrating meaning into developing adaptive behaviour. Results in personal growth.

Because people are unique and react in their own particular way, not everyone will go through all these stages. You need to be aware of them, however, as you can then help people to understand their reactions. Sometimes people will get stuck at one stage or encounter a setback and slip backwards, and you may need to help them to move on.

The diagram overleaf shows how peoples' level of self-esteem changes throughout the seven stages we have just looked at.

The death of a loved one is one of the most difficult unchosen transitions most people will face. But it is important to remember that people go through a grieving period over other losses, such as those connected with their job role, home or frustrated expectations, as well.

If someone is grieving over something which is difficult, but not terribly

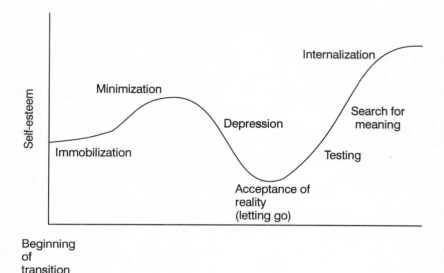

Figure 10.1 Self-esteem changes during transitions   *Source:* Kubler-Ross (1975)

traumatic (for example, they don't get a promotion they were expecting, or experience another job- or career-related loss) and you want to help them to move out of denial, a useful approach is to reflect back their statements of denial, and then add on a statement which indicates the opposite. For example, for a staff member whose largest client has changed over from your company to a new supplier you could say:

> You say you are hoping to convince Tom to hire us again, yet he has made it clear verbally, and twice in writing, that the decision to use Competitor X is final. Is it likely that he will change his mind now?

You could also challenge by asking where his/her time is better spent – on chasing Tom to change his mind, or chasing new business.

STRESS

Employee stress is one of the largest problems facing organizations today. Pressure and anxiety are common causes of poor performance at work. Having a general understanding of stress will help you to assist anxious staff. This section is intended to be a very simple framework to assist you in recognizing stress symptoms in staff, and in being knowledgeable both about the sources of stress and about effective ways of coping with it.

First, it is important to understand that sources of stress vary from person to person. What is stressful to one person may not be to another. Individuals vary not only in their perceptions of stressors, but also in their skills in managing stress, and in their confidence in their ability to cope with change. It is also important to remember that a certain – manageable – level of stress can be a positive motivating force.

Signs that staff are experiencing too much stress include:

- Decrease in productivity or performance.
- High level of lateness, sickness or absenteeism.
- High level of errors or accidents.
- Uncooperative behaviour.
- Excessive anger at minor irritations.
- Clashes with colleagues.
- Obvious tension or anxiety.
- A fatigued, weary, or despondent air.
- Inability to focus on the job at hand.
- Hyperactivity.
- Inability to slow down or relax.
- Lack of care for personal appearance.

Sources of stress can be internal, external, or a mixture of both. There can also be either temporary or ongoing problems which cause stress. Stress which is external comes from the environment or organization, and stress which is internal has to do with the individual's ability to cope with the demands placed upon him/her.

Problems which are often (but not always) external include:

- Too much change at once.
- Important changes which come as a surprise.
- Work overload (either too much to do, or too difficult to do).
- Work underload (boredom and too little stimulation are also stressful).
- Insufficient information for job to be performed effectively.
- Conflicts in demands placed upon him/her.
- Unrealistic objectives or time pressures.
- Organization has poor internal communications.
- Incompetent senior management.

- Organization weak in structure and procedures.
- Organization/culture/manager overly authoritarian or bureaucratic.
- Feeling of not being able to make a difference.
- Difficult relationship with boss or staff.
- Difficult relationships with colleagues (competition, not being able to share problems).
- Being unable to control, contain or remedy a situation.
- Important goals are made inaccessible.
- Regular but unpredictable crises (creating a state of negative expectation which is exhausting).
- Tedious work.
- Interruptions.
- Role conflict.
- Values, interests, or aims conflicting with others.
- Lack of personal control over things important to him/her.

The following graph of difficulty/ability zones is a useful visual representation for discussing work difficulty with staff. It demonstrates how competence in any specific context will depend upon the relationship between two perceptions: the perceived difficulty of the task and the perceived ability to achieve it (Elliot, 1993).

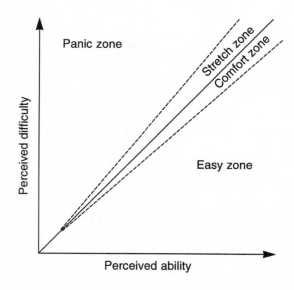

Figure 10.2 Difficulty/ability zones   *Source: Management Development*

Panic zone

Here the difficulty of the task is perceived to be well in excess of the individual's ability to achieve it. The reaction will probably be panic, anxiety and stress. Avoidance is likely, as is incompetent performance.

Stretch zone

The work is just a little more demanding than they think they can usually achieve. It poses a challenge, releases energy, and completion engenders a sense of achievement.

Comfort zone

The work is difficult enough to be challenging, yet within the employee's perceived ability to do it. Tasks are approached with zest and confidence.

Easy zone

The work appears easy and well within the employee's competence. Their reaction may well be boredom or lack of concentration.

Common internal problems include:

- Fear of being promoted and having to deal with new responsibilities.
- Lack of skill in interacting with people.
- Lack of confidence or low self-esteem.
- Inner fears and anxieties.
- Inability to listen.
- Fear of not being promoted or not meeting other goals.
- Anxiety about abilities.
- Being alone without support.
- Emotional overload (taking on others' problems).

Once the sources of stress have been identified, an important decision must be made: whether to remove or change the stressor (if possible), or whether to change the reactive coping mechanism(s). First, the employee needs to analyze the situations to assess what is changeable and what is not. Managing stress means consciously monitoring one's personal reactions to life and learning how to react positively (in terms of both thinking and behaviour) to change, other people, conflict, pressures, etc.

Positive ways of coping with stress are often ones in which the person tries to take control of the situation (attempting to affect either the stressor or the reaction), whereas negative ways of coping are often attempts to avoid a situation (avoid the stressor or avoid/repress the reaction). It generally feels better to do something about a situation than to feel like a victim, running away or hiding from it. However, there are times when attempting to control a situation is inappropriate, and avoiding it is not such a bad idea.

Coping strategies which are usually positive include:

- Trying to find out more about the situation.
- Social support (sharing problems with others).
- Trying to see the positive side of the situation.
- Making a plan of action and following it.
- Taking things one day at a time and one step at a time.
- Trying to step back from the situation and be more objective.
- Trying not to act too hastily or follow the first hunch.
- Learning how to relax.
- Constructive self-talk.
- Challenging cognitive distortion.
- Changing aggressive or passive behaviour.
- Balancing lifestyle.
- Time management.
- Emotional outlets (professional counselling, support from HR/personnel).
- Physical activities (exercise, sports, muscular relaxation, stamina building).

Coping strategies which are usually negative include:

- Taking problems/stress out on other people.
- Keeping feelings to self.
- Isolating (avoiding being with people).
- Denial.
- Alcohol.
- Overeating.
- Tranquillizing or recreational drugs.
- Self-delusion (distorting reality).
- Inappropriate humour.

By using facilitative techniques with stressed members of staff, you can help them to turn anxiety, fear, confusion, and indecision into challenge, opportunity, and effort. Help them to determine their sources of stress and their ways of coping, and to generate alternatives.

Organizational interventions to help employees with stress are often focused on the individual, and concentrate on modifying employees' reactions to stressful situations. There is, however, another level at which intervention is needed: addressing specific aspects of job and organizational design to find out where unproductive stress is generated, and then redesigning those areas.

11

Performance Management

THE PERFORMANCE MANAGEMENT SYSTEM

The term 'performance management' is often used to describe a revamped appraisal system or a performance-related bonus scheme. Performance management, though, needs to be looked at in the much larger and more comprehensive context of continuous improvement in business performance. The 'holistic' performance management system takes into account several ongoing and integrated processes, within the framework of achieving overall business strategy. Most of these processes involve using facilitation techniques.

The diagram overleaf demonstrates the interrelated nature of the individual aspects of performance management. Setting objectives leads to determining what human resources are needed to meet them, and what supports and resources these staff will need to meet their individual objectives. Then achievement and progress need to assessed, both formally and informally. The cycle continues as new objectives are planned and decisions are taken regarding how to allocate human resources in the future.

The performance management system promotes self-improvement at both the level of the individual and the organization. Thus, each aspect of the performance management system must be considered at both these levels. Objectives are set at the level of the organization (strategies) as well as at the level of the individual (how the individual will contribute to the strategies). Human resources needs are considered relative to the company's needs to promote, downsize, transfer or recruit, as well as on the individual level, where career aspirations are taken into account. Resources and support for achieving objectives must be procured for the company (information and communication technology, building space usage, large-scale training programmes, etc) as well as for individuals, who will have their own specific training, resources, coaching and counselling needs.

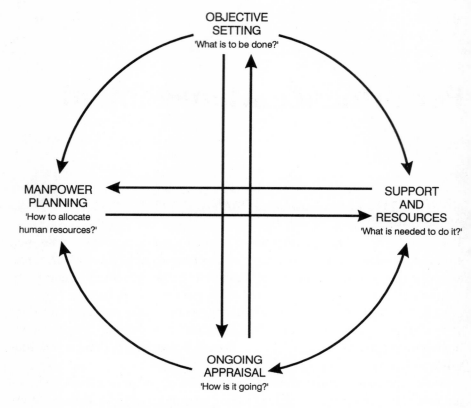

Figure 11.1 Performance management system

Appraisal must also take place at both levels, monitoring both organizational and individual capability.

There are two main areas of opportunity for facilitation when setting objectives. First, while corporate and departmental objectives will usually be determined by management (with or without employee input), you can facilitate your staff's thinking about how they are going to contribute to meeting the objectives. Second, you can facilitate their coming up with additional objectives of their own, as well as plans for meeting those and ways of measuring their progress and performance.

Facilitation techniques can be used to pinpoint the exact areas of developmental need, as well as for determining which modes of support will be most useful. For example, an employee might need to improve his/her supervisory skills, determining more precisely what exactly their difficulties are, and which particular supervisory skills are weak. The next step is to determine whether a training course, coaching, or counselling will be most helpful, or some combination of these. All too often, the response to a developmental need is to send the person on a course that *sounds* as if it will cover the topic. Using your facilitative skills will help you to ascertain the exact nature and depth of their need, and to determine together a method of learning which will be most suited to that need.

An organization's human resource planning should be performed alongside career planning for individuals. The supply and demand of human resources are matched correspondingly so that skills are utilized to the best possible advantage, and the aspirations of the individual are taken into account. This co-ordination of organizational and individual needs is becoming more commonplace as companies recognize that they need to make the best use of human resources, and that high staff turnover is expensive. This component of manpower planning is referred to as succession planning. Facilitation skills will come in useful during the part of the succession planning process which involves talking to your staff; in other words, during 'career counselling'.

APPRAISAL

The most effective appraisals meet all the needs of all the parties: the manager, the organization and the member of staff. In addition to being opportunities for managers to assess, develop and motivate, appraisals are an opportunity for staff to pursue their own issues and concerns.

The skills needed for conducting an appraisal include obtaining information, providing feedback, problem-solving, motivating and facilitating. Depending on the nature of the appraisal, these skills will be used in varying degrees, but all of the objectives above can best be achieved by using facilitation to some degree.

Nowadays, appraisals place heavy emphasis on the future. The process is less likely to be simply a manager's assessment of someone's past performance, as was common in the past. Instead, appraisals are now more likely to be mutually participative, which leads to a greater 'ownership' of the outcome on the part of the member of staff, and therefore makes them more likely to improve. The most effective way to do an appraisal is to have it focused mainly on the staff member: in other words, get them to do as much of it as possible themselves, which is synonymous with a facilitative style. This is too idealistic to be practicable in some cases, though. Although you want the appraisal to be as objective a process as possible, it is impossible and unproductive to have no judgements or opinions involved. However, since the success of the appraisal is extremely dependent on the employee's perception of its fairness, it is important to elicit and consider the person's thoughts. If appraisal schemes are not handled well, they can be *worse* than useless in that they can actually worsen both performance and working relationships.

One way to increase perceptions of the fairness of the appraisal is to rate everyone in similar positions according to the same criteria. Another way is to use facilitative techniques in order to get staff to air their views and concerns.

Specific areas in which facilitating will help you to perform an appraisal include:

- Putting the employee at ease if their body language indicates tension.
- Being aware of both your own and their likely feelings, which will help you to establish a rapport from the outset.
  - For the manager
    Positive feelings:
    — To be helpful and understanding to the member of staff
    — To be kind and tolerant to them
    — To motivate them
    Negative feelings:
    — Fear of carrying out the interview ineffectively and negatively affecting the working relationship
    — Fear of upsetting the person (if there is criticism to be given)
    — Fear of unleashing powerful emotions
  - For the member of staff
    Positive feelings:
    — To be liked and accepted by their boss
    — To get help with problems they have at work
    — To get suggestions for how to move forward
    Negative feelings:
    — Fear of criticism and punishment from their boss.

                                                              (de Board, 1985)

- Giving staff advance warning of appraisals and requesting that they think ahead about certain topics will help them to feel more prepared and confident and to know better what to expect.

Encourage the employee to discuss as many points as possible, and then probe the areas that they don't cover. Some staff may want your point of view instead (the 'that is what managers are paid for' attitude) but they are in a minority compared to people who would prefer to assess and constructively criticize themselves. People are sensitive to criticism from others and tend to reject it, even when it is justified and when there is valid proof or evidence. Operating in a facilitative style (trying to get *them* to discuss their own weaknesses) is often much more effective in getting them to consider seriously and accept areas which need improvement. A neutral scale on paper which you can both work from is a useful device to have. Below is a sample of such a scale, using teamwork as an example.

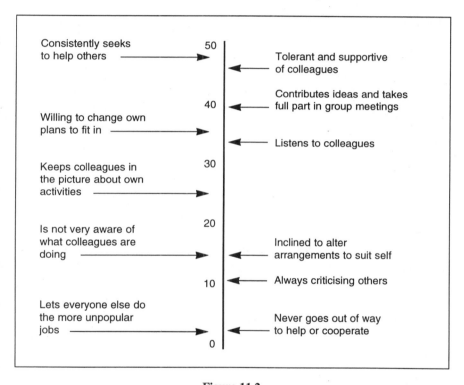

Figure 11.2

Source: This figure is taken from *Appraisal: Routes to Improved Performance* by Clive Fletcher, published by the Institute of Personnel and Development and reproduced with their permission.

If the main objectives of the appraisal are to enhance the person's motivation and development, then facilitative techniques must be used as much as possible. If the objective is to pass on information about poor performance, or to explain why a promotion is not being given, then facilitative skills are needed to help the employee determine how to improve or move forward once the feedback has been given.

Here are some suggested opening questions:

- How might you perform more effectively?
- What are the ways of achieving the necessary improvement?
- What are your development needs?
- What solutions do you recommend?
- How can we work together more effectively to improve your performance?
- Describe the situations where your job goes well.
- Describe the situations where your job does not go well.
- What aspects of the job are difficult?
- What objectives have not been met?
- What changes or challenges are likely to occur in the near future?
- Where do you feel satisfied with your efforts? (Ask for examples.)
- Where do you not feel satisfied with your efforts? (Ask for examples.)
- What are your career aspirations? Ask about any new aims or interests, and any changes which have occurred since your last discussion.
- What are your feelings about the position and your future potential?

RISING TO OPPORTUNITIES

This book has focused a lot on helping staff deal with difficulties and address problems. At times management can feel like endless fire-fighting and trouble-shooting. However, it is vital not to forget the positive applications of developing others. Unfortunately, the image of words like 'coaching' and 'counselling' is that they are connected with poor performers – with those who are *not* succeeding. This image is beginning to change as more companies are recognizing the value of these activities in helping average performers and even high flyers to improve their performance further.

Facilitative coaching and counselling are ideal ways of assisting others to reach their full potential in situations where the individual concerned does not even recognize the extent of their potential. Women in particular often underestimate their own potential. It may not ever occur to them to consider some of the possibilities open to them. For example, the managing director of a large screening centre in London complained that he wanted to move competent women upwards into more senior management positions, but that several of the women he wanted to promote did not want to move up because the positions did not match their own ideas about themselves. He expressed frustration at wanting more diverse and competent management and yet being unable to achieve this, partly due to self-esteem issues. Here was a perfect opportunity to apply facilitative coaching/counselling in a very positive way.

A 'modern' manager should be convinced that the main way of adding value to the organization is to help their staff to learn, grow and develop. Facilitative development means creating conditions which allow people to perform to the best of their ability. The manager who acts as a facilitative coach thinks of delegation as an opportunity to provide learning experiences. Instead of selecting someone who can already do the work being delegated, they deliberately select someone who cannot do it. In addition to setting the objectives of the actual work to be done, they add learning goals. Of course, risks have to be carefully calculated. For each assignment or task, the manager must bear in mind the potential benefits of success to the individual and the organization, the potential cost of a mistake, and the balance of probability between success and failure.

PRE-DISCIPLINARY ACTION

The term *pre*-disciplinary is used because facilitative techniques are not a substitute for disciplinary action. Instead, they can precede and complement disciplinary action. Using these techniques at a sufficiently early stage can often prevent the need for disciplinary action from arising; using them along with the formal disciplinary procedure can help people to take ownership of and responsibility for resolving the problem.

CASE EXAMPLE 8

A normally polite and pleasant software support service representative was known to have a personal problem which was making him edgy and sharper than usual when dealing with people. This behaviour continued and deteriorated to the extent that his approach to customers became unacceptable and initial disciplinary steps had to be taken. Some counselling from his manager when a problem first became apparent would perhaps have eliminated the necessity for more drastic action.

Personal problems, of course, should remain private unless the person is willing to talk or the situation is adversely affecting their work. In fact, managers may feel uncomfortable about initiating a conversation with someone whose work has not yet been very adversely affected. However, if attempting to tackle the problem early might avoid its getting much worse, then it is worth giving it a try. If your offer is rejected, do not push. Simply point out that the situation cannot be allowed to continue indefinitely if it is affecting the company negatively, and continue to monitor performance. You can then offer help again later on.

Pre-disciplinary meetings fall into different categories. Sometimes you have the facts, while at other times you need to do some investigatory work. If you have the facts then you need first to communicate the problem clearly and concisely. Then use your facilitation skills to try to establish agreement on the existence of the problem, and to help the employee to decide on some appropriate courses of action. Do not ask too many questions before you tell them your reasons for calling the meeting, or you will appear furtive.

Pre-disciplinary meetings can be difficult because of the emotional content. In response to your statement of the problem(s), you are likely to get an emotional outburst, denial of a problem, or deflections away from your point. Listen to the emotional outburst and let them take their time. Acknowledge their feelings and reflect back the emotional content. Do not make any judgements about their feelings: don't say, 'You are right (or wrong) to feel upset/angry'; try, 'you are upset/angry about that'.

In order to avoid getting caught up in their deflections, you need to have a very clear idea of what the issue is and be sure to keep coming back to it. Reflection can also be used in a pre-disciplinary situation to play back any ridiculous statements that someone makes in defence of themselves. Often they will then admit they are not being straightforward. For example, if someone with high absenteeism brings up her new puppy when you refer to her attendance record, you could say: 'Your puppy has stopped you from coming to work regularly over the past few months?' This is likely to make her appreciate the weakness of the excuse.

12

Organizational Applications

CHANGE MANAGEMENT

In order to create a competitive advantage, companies need to be flexible about changing at the same time as maintaining the highest possible level of performance and productivity from employees. Implementing positive strategies to ease the pressures of upheaval and uncertainty is absolutely necessary. Given people's resistance to and natural fear of change, managing it is not an easy task. Employees will require help in coping with and adjusting to changes.

Not only do managers need to facilitate in order to support and motivate staff during periods of change, they also need to play an active role in creating the new environment. Many companies are changing – for the better – from being downwardly operating, hierarchical, directive and slow to change to being upwardly operating, flatter, 'empowering' and more flexible. Using facilitative techniques is essential in order to effectively *implement* this cultural change (rather than just paying it lip service), so an ideal time to institute the top-down training of managers in facilitation is as part of a change management programme.

TEAM BUILDING

Facilitation skills are also used to help groups in problem-solving, decision-making, and conflict resolution. Here are some of the aspects of group process which can be addressed (Kolb, Rubin, McIntyre, 1984):

- Goals or mission
    - How clearly defined are the goals?
    - Who sets the goals?
    - How much agreement is there among members concerning the goals?
    - How much commitment?

— How clearly measurable is goal achievement?
— How do group goals relate to broader organizational goals? To personal goals?
- Group norms
- Leadership
- Decision-making
  — How does it happen?
  — Is everyone satisfied with how it happens?
  — Is there a better way?
- Role expectations
  — Role ambiguity – are people clear about their own and others' roles within the team?
  — Role conflict – do any team members feel pulled in different directions due to dual or multiple roles?
  — Role overload – are the responsibilities of the roles manageable?

MOTIVATING HIGH FLYERS

In the past, many large organisations had "fast track" programmes which identified and developed exceptional individuals for specific senior positions in their companies. Today, with restructuring, downsizing, and de-layering, organisations can rarely groom people for specific positions. The emphasis has shifted to supported self-development where everyone is expected to contribute to the maximum of their ability and drive their own careers. However, organisations are recognising that they still need to invest in developing in their future leaders. Today's high potential programmes help prepare individuals for senior manager and executive roles but do not guarantee specific posts. (Human Resource Partnership, 1997)

These programmes identify and develop individuals with high potential and equip them with the knowledge, skills and behaviours (competencies) necessary to ensure the continuing success of the company. The individual's personal development plans are aligned with both the company's business goals and the individual's needs.

Reasons why organizations have high-potential programmes include:

- Ensuring the supply of effective business leaders in the future.
- Developing a shared understanding of the key business issues facing the organization and what needs to be done to succeed in the future.

- Ensuring that the senior managers/executives of the future are equipped with the skills and abilities needed to succeed in a changing environment.
- Keeping key employees motivated and committed to the organization.
- Acting as a catalyst for change in attitudes/behaviour.

Key stakeholders within the organization are responsible for programme design, as well as for the communication and actual implementation of it. The process of participant selection is open in that all employees will know how they can be nominated and what it involves. Programme success is evaluated at regular intervals and feedback is acted upon.

Programme development activities might include a combination of any of the following:

- Specific programmes/workshops designed to accelerate development in the senior manager competences.
- Existing internal and external training/development programmes.
- Using opportunities in current role to develop differentiating competences.
- Taking up opportunities in other departments/functions.

Support for high-potential programme participants also takes a variety of forms; for example, scheduling review meetings with sponsors/human resources staff, learning partner groups, action learning sets, internal and/or external mentors, and allocating time and resources for personal development.

However, the underlying concept behind a high-potential programme is 'self-managed learning'. The individual will drive his/her own development under the programme with support as needed: 'Individuals are much more likely to regard organisational change in a positive light if they associate change with learning, and are already enthusiastic about their own personal development.' (Phillips, 1994) Enthusiasm for change is easiest to stimulate if people are visibly supported, helped and encouraged in the self-learning process by their manager and by the organization. Attitudes and behaviours which a participant must take on include:

- Assertiveness – making it clear what they want to achieve.
- Taking initiatives – requesting help from others when needed.
- Openness and honesty – expressing their reasons for doing (or not doing) specific tasks.
- Asking for feedback and suggestions – prompting others to give a full view of their successes and mistakes.

- Networking – taking all available opportunities to build useful networks.
- Clarifying objectives – the project should have a clear, written statement of objectives.
- Taking responsibility – above all, participants need to take responsibility for their own learning.

CONSULTING/CUSTOMER SERVICE

Facilitative techniques are extremely useful for working with clients as well as with staff. Of course, as a consultant you can't use an exclusively facilitative style (usually you have been hired to give information), but you can use listening and questioning skills when interviewing to get as much 'real' information as possible, and then again after presenting your findings in order to help your client to find ways of using what you have discovered.

ENTREPRENEURISM/INTRAPRENEURISM

Venture capitalists, bankers, small business and business start-up consultants and managers whose staff are intrapreneurs (managing start-up ventures within the organization) can all benefit from applying facilitative techniques to help the entre- or intrapreneur. Developing and guiding entrepreneurs requires a balance of high support levels along with a high level of challenge.

The concept of 'ownership' of the business idea, plan or approach to problem resolution is especially applicable to entrepreneurs, who tend to see their business as 'their baby' and have difficulty accepting outside advice.

- Use listening skills to build trust and get them to open up, and to detect problem areas which they may be initially reluctant to reveal.
- Challenge in a pulling fashion in order to get them to consider rather than defend. This will also help them to take action when they are blocked.
- Work through decision-making and problem-solving processes with entrepreneurs, so that they can then continue to use these themselves and with their own staff.

ORGANIZATIONAL DEVELOPMENT

In order for the organization to develop, effective training in facilitation will need to be introduced as a normal part of its mainstream management development programme. In order for the subsequent use of facilitation to be effective, however, the company culture needs to really support the use of these skills; in other words, it must *really* value its people. Otherwise, facilitation skills will be used manipulatively, causing even more underlying problems.

Every organization has an unstated culture consisting of unwritten rules and norms which guide how people are expected to behave. It is essential that the organization's unspoken messages to employees match up with and back up its spoken messages. Unwritten beliefs and rules (even though often only based on tradition) are very difficult to change, but they have at least as much – if not more – effect on employee behaviour than do spoken and written rules.

Two aspects of culture to monitor for 'health' include:

1. People's receptiveness to 'problems'.
   — Is bad news shared, or is there a tendency to 'shoot the messenger'?
   — Is admitting to feeling stressed tantamount to admitting weakness, failure, or lack of capability?
   — Are staff and managers openly rewarded for bringing up problems and difficulties rather than for burying their heads?
2. The way that conflict is handled within the organization.
   — Is conflict viewed as negative?
   — Is the environment overcompetitive? Is conflict seen as a situation in which one side must win rather than an opportunity for learning and growth? In such a climate, everyone is out for themselves, feeling a bit paranoid, always protecting themselves, being defensive and passing the buck
   — Is conflict repressed, or smoothed over and avoided? Problems may be avoided temporarily, but under the surface there is anger, discomfort and frustration
   — Alternatively, are people always questioning in a non-blaming manner, looking for ways to improve? If managed properly, conflict can be an important source of new ideas and approaches.

Unstated messages about leadership can be communicated through the ways in which managers are appraised and remunerated, in who is actually promoted and who is spoken well of. It is important to consider how managers will be rewarded for making changes. Will managers really be rewarded or will they be subtly penalized for developing their employees? For example, is there a payoff for managers who empower and develop their staff to the point where they leave the department and move on to something else? Is the achievement acknowledged from above? Or does the manager's own department simply suffer from the loss? People are very much aware of what behaviour they will, in reality, be rewarded for, versus what is said to be rewarded.

References

Ahern J 'Counselling's Added Value', *Counselling At Work*, British Association for Counselling, Autumn 1993.

Allison T (1991) Counselling and Coaching, *The Handbook of Performance Management*, Institute of Personnel and Development, London.

Anderson G 'From Performance Appraisal to Performance Management', *Training and Development*, October 1993.

Berryman J (1991) *Developmental Psychology and You*, The British Psychological Society & Routledge, London.

Blackler F and Shimmin S (1984) *Applying Psychology In Organisations*, Methuen, London & New York.

Blake R and Mouton J (1964) *The Managerial Grid*, Gulf Publishing Co.

Caudron S 'Delegate for results', *Industry Week (USA)*, February 1995.

CEPEC (1988) *Counselling at Work, Introducing and Using The Skills*, Kogan Page, London.

CEPEC (1992) *Life and Career – A Self-Development Workbook*, CEPEC, London.

Charles-Edwards D 'Human Leadership and Counselling in Organisations', *Counselling At Work*, British Association for Counselling, Summer 1993.

Clutterbuck D and Megginson D (1995) *Mentoring In Action*, Kogan Page, London.

Collins JC and Porras JI (1996) *Built to Last*, Century, London.

The Conference Board, *Does Quality Work? A Review of Relevant Studies*, New York, Brussells, Ottawa 1993.

Cunningham I 'Someone to Watch Over Me', *Human Resources*, Winter 1992/3.

de Board R (1983) *Counselling People at Work*, Gower Publishing Co. Ltd, Hants UK.

Duhig Berry Ltd, *People Management & Prince*, NCC Blackwell, 1992.

Durcan J and Oates D (1994) *The Manager As Coach*, Pitman Publishing, London.

Egan G (1990) *Exercises in Helping Skills*, Brooks/Cole Co., California USA.

Elliot K 'Managerial Competencies', *Management Development*, November 1993.

Feldman D (1988) *Managing Careers in Organisations*, Scott, Foresman and Co., Boston, MA.

Fletcher C (1993) *Appraisal: Routes to Improved Performance*, Institute of Personnel and Development, London.

Fowler A 'How to Manage Cultural Change', *Personnel Management Plus*, November 1993.

Fowler A 'How to Provide Effective Feedback', *People Management*, Vol. 2 No.14, 1996.

Geldard D (1993, 2nd ed) *Basic Personal Counselling*, Prentice Hall, New Jersey.

Glass N (1991) *Pro-active Management*, Cassell Educational Ltd, London.

Holdsworth R (1991) Appraisal, *The Handbook of Performance Management*, Institute of Personnel and Development, London.

Hopson B and Adams J (1976) *Transition: Understanding & Managing Personal Change*, Martin Robertson.

Human Resource Partnership (1997) *High Potential Programmes*, London.

Johnson D (1992) 'Counselling Business Start-ups and Owner-managers of Small Firms', *Employee Counselling Today*, Vol. 4, Issue 1.

Kolb D, Rubin I and McIntyre J (1984) *Organisational Psychology*, Prentice Hall, New Jersey.

Kubler-Ross E (1975) *Death: The Final Stage of Growth*, Prentice Hall, New Jersey.

Landsberg M (1986) *The Tao of Coaching*, HarperCollins, London.

Lee F (1993) 'Stress', *Personnel Today*, 7 December.

Lester S 'Appraising the Performance Appraisal', *Training and Development*, November 1993.

Lewis E (1970) *The Psychology of Counselling*, Holt, Rinehart and Winston Inc., NY.

Lockett J (1992) *Effective Performance Management*, Kogan Page, London.

The Mental Health Foundation, *Someone to Talk to at Work*, London, 1989.

Mumford A (1993) *Management Development – Strategies for Action*, Institute of Personnel and Development, London.

Munroe EA, Manthei RJ and Small JJ (1983) *Counselling, A Skills Approach*, Methuen Publications (New Zealand) Ltd.

Neale F (1991) *The Handbook of Performance Management*, Institute of Personnel and Development, London.

Nelson-Jones R (1992) *Practical Counselling and Helping Skills*, Cassell Education Ltd, London.

Nickols FW 'Feedback about Feedback', *Human Resource Development Quarterly*, Vol. 6, No. 3, 1995.

Nicodemus R 'Facilitating Teamwork', *Counselling At Work*, British Association for Counselling, Winter 1993.

Payne J and Payne S (1994) *Letting Go Without Losing Control: How to Delegate and Do More*, Pitman, London.

Pease A (1992, 17th ed) *Body Language*, Sheldon Press, London.

Pedler M, Burgoyne J and Boydell T (1986) *A Manager's Guide to Self-Development*, McGraw-Hill, London.

Phillips N (1995) *Motivating For Change*, Pitman, London.

Phillips R 'Coaching for Higher Performers', *The Ashridge Journal*, April 1994.

Pitts G 'Employee Assistance Programs', *Insight*, No. 19, June 1993.

Pokras S (1989) *Systematic Problem-Solving and Decision-Making*, Kogan Page, London.

Reddy M (1987) *The Manager's Guide to Counselling At Work*, Routledge (published in association with the British Psychological Society), London.

Robin-Evenden F 'Coaching and the Development Relationship', *Training and Development*, April 1994.

Sadler P and Milner K (1993) *The Talent – Intensive Organisation*, Economist Intelligence Unit, London.

Salisbury FS (1994) *Developing Managers as Coaches*, McGraw Hill, London.

Segerman-Peck L (1991) *Networking and Mentoring*, Piatkus, London.

Shaw RB (1997) *Building the High Trust Organisation*, Jossey-Bass Inc., San Francisco.

Smith M and Vickers T, 'And What About the Survivors?', *Training and Development*, January 1994.

Smith P 'An Intervention Assessment Model for Managers', *Counselling At Work*, British Association for Counselling, Winter 1993.

Steele T 'Preparing for the Worst', *Human Resources*, Summer 1993.

Tannenbaum T and Schmidt WH 'How to Choose a Leadership Style', *Harvard Business Review Monograph*, March-April 1958.

Thomas M 'What You Need to Know About Business Process Re-Engineering', *Personnel Management*, January 1994.

Thorne P (1989) *The New General Manager*, McGraw-Hill, London.

Timperley S and Sisson K (1989) 'From Manpower Planning to Human Resource Planning'. In *Personnel Management in Britain* K Sisson ed., Basil Blackwell, Oxford.

Torrington D and Hall L (1991) *Personnel Management*, Prentice Hall, New Jersey.

Tyson S (1997) *The Practice of Human Resource Strategy*, Pitman, London.

Wallum P (1991) Succession Management, *The Handbook of Performance Management*, Institute of Personnel and Development, London.

Whetten DA, Cameron K and Woods M (1996) *Effective Empowerment and Delegation*, Harper Collins, London.

Wright B 'Surviving Downsizing', *Counselling At Work*, British Association for Counselling, Winter 1993.

Index